The above sentiment, chalked on the flank of a locomotive awaiting the scrapping torch, was probably written by a melancholy railroad man or a despondent railfan. Such phrases as "goodbye, old pal," or "so long, my friend," have also been discovered among the ranks of condemned steam engines.

THE TWILIGHT OF STEAM LOCOMOTIVES

THE TWILIGHT OF STEAM LOCOMOTIVES

By RON ZIEL

GROSSET & DUNLAP   *Publishers*   **NEW YORK**

"HOW ARE THE MIGHTY FALLEN!"

II Samuel 1:19

ACKNOWLEDGEMENTS

In the course of preparing a volume dealing with a subject as extensive as the demise of the steam locomotive, an author may expect to rely on the time and efforts of many others. The following persons, all of whom the author has met or carried on extensive correspondence with, have been largely responsible for this book in its final form. I am deeply indebted to them for their services: Freeman Hubbard, for offering helpful suggestions and opening the extensive files of *Railroad Magazine* to the author; David P. Morgan, who offered early encouragement and his own fine writings on the steam locomotive; Alfred G. Wilson, and Carl F. Graves for their technical aid; Lucius Beebe, for granting the use of certain of his writings; H. F. Brown, for giving of his time and knowledge to lend great assistance in the field of motive power comparison; E. L. Pardee, president of the National Railway Historical Society, who guided the author's efforts at critical moments; Charles E. Fisher, president of the Railway and Locomotive Historical Society, who proffered timely criticism; M. H. Klebolt, president of the Illini Railroad Club, for his liaison with the Burlington R.R.; John W. Barriger, president of the Pittsburgh & Lake Erie Railroad, who aided in the field of motive power; T. W. M. Long, president of the Reader Railroad, whose Southern hospitality was abundant; Paul W. Dillon, Chairman of the Board of Northwestern Steel & Wire Co., for revealing the somber scrapping process to the author's camera; F. Nelson Blount, for his assistance on the "Steamtown" portion; Lt. Col. Margaret E. Schulten and Lt. Ed Hurley who were responsible for the author's successful sojourn to Fort Eustis; Jim Pearce, a Rio Grande road foreman who accompanied the author on his narrow-gauge wanderings; Dean Albert Christ-Janer, the Art School, Pratt Institute, who assured the Institute's backing of the project; The Operating and Public Relations departments of many railroads mentioned within; The Interstate Commerce Commission and the Association of American Railroads for supplying valuable resource material; Marshall Gatewood Moseley, who traveled with the author and offered valuable artistic advice throughout the development of the book; John Dexter Leland, whose art and typing experience proved helpful; J. Arthur Johnsen, who also aided in the completion of this work; Jerry Goodwin, who accompanied the author in Mexico and portions of the South; Robert Ziel, the author's brother, who also traveled with him and helped in many ways. The author is especially appreciative of his parents, who encouraged the venture, morally and financially, from its early inception.

TABLE OF CONTENTS

Left: Bevier & Southern 2-8-2 struggling uphill with coal tonnage.
Title page: Double-headed T-1 4-8-4's on a Reading steam special.

INTRODUCTION

Of the many facets of the entire subject of railroading, a locomotive under steam was the most attractive. It may have represented a technological achievement of specialized engineering design or it may have been among the simplest of man's industrial machines. In motion or at rest it was animate to an incomprehensible degree, and every locomotive had its own distinctive characteristics and personality. Rarely, if ever, have any two engines built from the same blueprints had the same performance and operating qualities, and no locomotive could be run efficiently if the engineer were not alert and sensitive to its individual peculiarities. It is with sharp insight that the British call their engineers "drivers" for the term "iron horse" is not merely a poetic fancy, but a recognition of these animate qualities.

The past two centuries have witnessed more changes in human society and economic environment than in all of previous history. Among the technical advances it is hard to find any machine that so symbolizes the Industrial Revolution as the steam locomotive. Deriving great power from one parent, the stationary steam engine, and great mobility from the other parent, the horse-drawn tramway, this offspring of many engineering skills can be considered as the most representative, as well as the most romantic, achievement of the Industrial Age.

In 1825 there was one steam locomotive in the United States, operated as an experiment by Col. John Stevens on a circle of track in Hoboken. Ninety-nine years later the steam locomotive census reached its peak with over 65,000 owned by Class One railroads, plus the uncounted thousands operating on short lines and industrial, terminal and logging roads. The next year, 1925, began the decline, and by some strange coincidence the first diesel was listed by the Association of American Railroads that same year.

Many studies have been made and much has been written about the disappearance of the steam locomotive, but the hard facts of economics, highway competition and improved steam locomotive technology brought the decline to 40,041 locomotives in 1940. The spec-

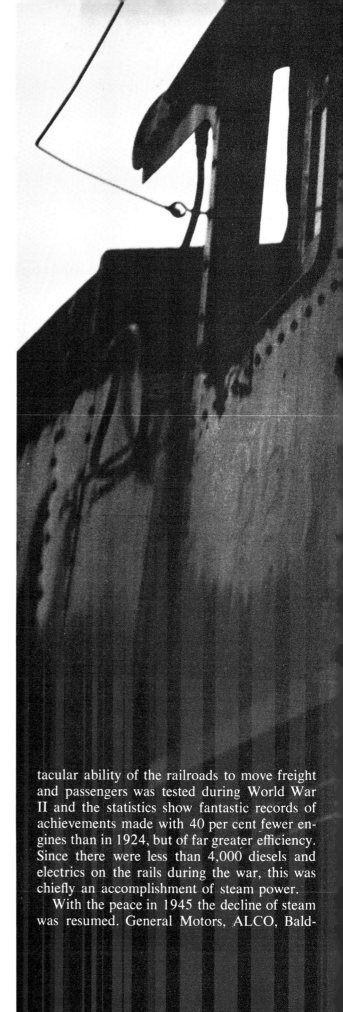

tacular ability of the railroads to move freight and passengers was tested during World War II and the statistics show fantastic records of achievements made with 40 per cent fewer engines than in 1924, but of far greater efficiency. Since there were less than 4,000 diesels and electrics on the rails during the war, this was chiefly an accomplishment of steam power.

With the peace in 1945 the decline of steam was resumed. General Motors, ALCO, Bald-

are museum pieces or are awaiting the scrapper's torch.

With steam all but extinct on the main lines, a diligent and dedicated search was necessary to find what remained on the short lines and the "little railroads." It is practically impossible to track down and report on every remaining steam locomotive. Such a listing and picture-taking would be quite repetitious and even dull, for the racers and the heavy haulers that were the most romantic and impressive are now gone, leaving only a few "work horses" on class-two and class-three railroads.

It is no wonder that the "iron horse" attracts a large group of enthusiasts. Among their number none is more active and zealous than Ron Ziel. This is his book and a personal document, for it is a record of a trans-continental search for surviving steam locomotives by an artist whose very youth made this book possible. Only a young man would have the energy to range more than 55,000 miles across 47 states and into Canada and Mexico in 16 months and the endurance to stay for weeks at a time on the road, flushing out the last steam engines in the bayous of Dixie, the forests of the Northwest and the factory yards of New England. One memorable journey, in the company of Marshall G. Moseley, a college friend, covered 15,000 miles by rail and highway in four weeks, and the air lines got no revenue from this railfan! In 1961 the first ideas were committed to film and paper during his senior year at Pratt Institute, where only two miles away the Brooklyn Eastern District Terminal's eccentricities of saddle-tankers and rights-of-way occupied by parked automobiles, aroused his earlier memories of the steam power which thundered on the high iron through the suburban towns along the Long Island Rail Road of his boyhood.

Perhaps in other times this might have been the record of a companion of Jason or a hundred other such seekers of a treasure, but in the middle of our century Ron Ziel has completed a different quest. This was more than an effort to make a picture report of the last remaining steam locomotives. It is a valedictory prepared by a young man who feels a sense of personal loss and an awareness of the very real passing of an era.

ALFRED G. WILSON

win-Lima-Hamilton, General Electric, Fairbanks-Morse and others began mass-producing diesel locomotives like automobiles, and the fate of the steam locomotive was inevitable. In 1952, with more diesels and ever fewer steam locomotives, the lines on the graph crossed and ten years later, in 1962, there were less than one hundred surviving steam engines in the Association of American Railroads listing of Class One roads. Few of these can operate and most

MECHANICAL SPLENDOR

Few who have ever watched the valve gear and side rods of a steam locomotive in action could seriously argue that the Industrial Revolution created any more fascinating machine. The engine room of a steam ship is quite interesting, as is a dynamo or a highspeed printing press; but what action compares to the opposed motions of main rod and eccentric crank, or the combination lever chasing the crosshead back and forth along the crosshead guide?

Here is power one can see. Deceptively the locomotive bellows and complains as the throttle is eased out. It seems that those slender rods and slim spoked wheels could never move so ponderous a weight as the engine alone, to say nothing of the thousands of tons of passenger or freight cars behind. Slowly the wheels turn. They may slip a little, but presently traction grips the rails. Surely the frail main rod will snap under the great stress of more than 200 pounds per square inch of boiler pressure going to work. As usual, however, the engine operates perfectly, and within minutes she is playfully obeying the laws of physics as she gathers mileage on the main. She may have balked and been annoyed at starting, but now it may take

two miles to stop her with the brakes on full emergency!

As the engine overcomes momentum and settles into her stride, little smoke is visible, for she is running at her designed efficiency speed. Now one can ponder the "monkey motion" as the aggregation of links, levers, bars and rods dance everywhere across the huge drivers in orderly fashion. Now the incongruity of equating hundreds of tons of steel with scores of miles per hour slowly resolves itself, and one can only marvel at such a machine, beguilingly female in her prim delicacy, yet overwhelmingly powerful and rugged.

Here one of the last surviving Pacifics which once rolled to Key West on the Florida East Coast, proudly shows off her Walschaert's gear at the Miami Railway Historical Society's Museum. Typical of the well-proportioned little Pacifics built for virtually all American railroads during the '20's, 4-6-2 No. 153 once steamed Flagler Specials over the line that went "out of sight of land by Pullman car." Automobiles now tread the F E C's fabled mainline to Key West, but 153 is the living link with Florida's fabulous early boom and the redoubtable Henry Flagler, developer, railroader and builder of the Sunshine State.

To have been present at the yards on a crisp
Autumn morning and to have observed the in-
describable bond between man and machine
as a mighty steam locomotive was roused for
a long day's labor was to witness the deepest
attachment of man to his calling. For all her
hundreds of tons of weight and thousands of
horsepower, the steam engine was a fragile
thing requiring care to the point of pampering.
No more lacking in fallibilities than are human
beings, steam engines had to be constantly attended. Every roundhouse had its force of hostlers; men who saw to the engines' every needs.
The hostlers wiped, oiled, cleaned and even
"exercised" the locomotives by running them
out of their stalls occasionally, to keep them in
prime operating condition. All night a man
would go from one engine to another, checking
their fires and feeding them coal and water.
Seeming to enjoy all this attention, the locomotives percolated away their resting hours; quite
content to just blow off a little steam whenever
disposed to do so.

Perhaps this was the true drama of the steam
age: the engine wiper who anxiously acquired
seniority for a chance to fire; then that day of
days when he became an engineer — the old
story of success in railroading, and a true one,
often repeated. It has been said that no two
locomotives, even those of the same series,
built on the same erecting floor, ever performed
in the same way. Like sisters, or even twins,
each engine had its own personality and its own
way of working; to the extent that crews had
their own favorites, or locomotives which were
actually feared. Such a "hoodoo" was Casey
Jones' Illinois Central 4-6-0 No. 382. After
killing three more men, it was finally scrapped.

Left: Burlington 0-5 Northern at Cicero, Illinois.
Above: Virginia Blue Ridge 0-6-0 at Tye River, Va.

"*...if anyone has bolted together a mechanism with just fifty per cent of the steam locomotive's solid spiritual satisfaction, he hasn't filed for a patent yet.*"

— DAVID P. MORGAN

When the tranquil countryside was disturbed by the diminutive locomotives of the 1830's, many a good citizen feared trouble of all sorts from the snorting intruders. Soon, however, artists were including a distant train with its characteristic plume of smoke on their canvases. Like the clipper ship and the Conestoga wagon, the steam car had become a device of man's not offensive to the natural beauty it traversed. In a precious few remote valleys and obscure factory yards the inspiration of artists from the nineteenth-century impressionists to the abstract expressionists still creates a memorable tribute to man's harmony with nature.

Only a few personalities of American story and song were equal to the steam-age railroad man in popularity and the intangible qualities by which folk music and legends are propagated. The pioneer, the cowboy, the nineteenth-century volunteer fireman and the soldiers of varied conflicts are probably the few peers of the men of all nationalities and races who sweat through the noonday heat laying rail across a continent or outran their destinies in an aura of flame and steam by night.

Little more than a decade ago, most boys still dreamed of opening the throttle on a manifest freight or an express passenger train as they pondered the antics of a little tinplate toy locomotive careening around the Christmas tree. Today few youngsters pay attention to railroading, and toy-department managers report sales of electric trains rapidly declining in recent years. The prevalent shoddy standards of toy train manufacture and the dramatic dash into space exploration are not the only reasons that young boys grasp at the virtually unattainable goal of being a space pilot instead of the palpable reality of running a locomotive. Just watch a youngster at the station when Reading's 2102 is due with a fan special. After the initial dismay of his first encounter with a steam engine, see the emotions of bygone childhoods reborn in the first generation to come of age since the diesel. Current railroad motive power offers no challenge to a generation out of touch with any stimuli greater than a television commercial. In fact, even a small bulldozer is more fascinating than the Electro-Motive Corporation's machine. All of the excitement of the steam engine is banished by the diesel's slick hood, which emits only a monotonous growl, while occasionally bleating like a lamb beset by wolves.

Few youngsters, however, are fortunate enough to encounter spinning drive wheels propelled by steam. They are more apt to discover a gargantuan mass of silent steel, the view of which is filtered by a wire fence. Perhaps at a museum, the boys and girls are allowed into the cab of a preserved steam locomotive. The children who clamber about such an engine can only sit in the cab and imagine the times when a roaring fire converted tons of coal and thousands of gallons of water into terrain-conquering power. Now they see only a few feet of track beyond the engine pilot. The pressure gauges have dropped to zero for the last time. These little fellows see only immovable steel, leaving all else to fancy. Someday they may be among the hundreds who line the tracks each time the Union Pacific or the Burlington runs an excursion behind their famed 4-8-4's. Then they may understand.

Left: Reader Railroad 2-6-2 in Arkansas.
Right: Long Island 4-6-0 at Stonybrook.

MAINTAINING A LOCOMOTIVE

When the steam locomotive was responsible for moving the nation's freight and the rapid transport of passengers, tens of thousands of railroad men were charged with repair and maintenance duties; keeping the big engines running. When one of those improbable machines was sent hurtling down steel rails on wheels held to the track by mere inches of flange, a loose rod or cracked axle could pre-cipitate a major disaster. Especially on the heavily-traveled mainlines, servicing standards were high and engines kept in an excellent state of repair.

Locomotives were dispatched from engine-houses to move trains over their divisions. It was in the enginehouse that the elaborate servicing facilities were located. At the end of a run a locomotive was uncoupled from her train and sent to the roundhouse, where engine maintenance was in constant process. Men would grease the running gear with alemite guns, wipe the rods, clean the fire and make minor adjustments on everything from faulty gauges to feed-water heaters, ever mindful that the turnaround time must be rapid enough to meet the engine's next assignment. After a few hours of quick but thorough checking and adjusting, the locomotive would be rolled over to the ready track; refueling and watering en route. Roaring under high pressure, she would join other engines awaiting clearance.

When the engineer and fireman arrived, they observed a strict ritual of checking their locomotive before departure. Whether running a slow drag freight or a sleek passenger engine, certain duties were common to the routines of all enginemen. The roundhouse crew may have spent much time on a locomotive, but it remained for the engine crew to make the final adjustments which ensured a safe journey.

On these pages this timeless routine is performed by the engineer and fireman of the Monadnock, Steamtown, and Northern's 2-8-0, No. 15, one of the operating engines which supplied the motive power for "Steamtown" at Keene, New Hampshire.

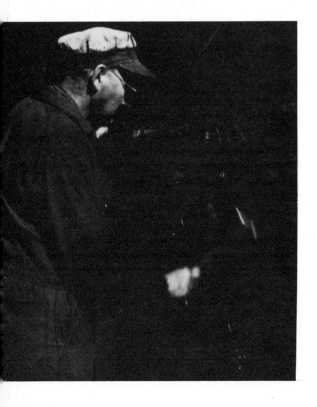

ENGINEER'S CHECK

Here engineer Clyde Sessions begins his chores. While the fireman stokes the fire, the engineer oils and checks the running gear. First he walks all around the engine, tapping every nut which could have been loosened by the vibrations of previous runs. Next, he tends to the grease cups and armed with the traditional oil can, deftly applies drops of the blue-brown fluid where required.

SPIT AND POLISH

After all of the mechanical devices are in good order, large wads of cotton waste are produced from beneath a seat in the cab and the crew completes their preparations for the day which will see the Consolidation make two round trips up the North Walpole branch of the Boston & Maine. At *right,* fireman Dave Barnes, on hand to play hostler on his day off, works at polishing the brass bell. At *lower right,* the engine has been coupled to her train. While passengers are boarding the old cars, a few last swabs of cotton waste are used to polish the headlight glass and siderods. The tender has been filled with coal and water. After testing the brakes, engineer Sessions runs his train up the line past the scenic grandeur of Mount Monadnock. The engine, which came from the Rahway Valley Railroad in New Jersey, is a Baldwin product of 1916. She provided the power for the 1962 season.

FIREMAN'S CHECK

Once the fire has been banked, fireman George Bartholomew fills the airpump oil reservoirs (*above*) and returns to his fire. Shaking down the grates (*right*), he uses a hose to ensure cleanliness. The fire is dependent upon a smooth constant flow of air up through the grates.

STEAMTOWN, U.S.A.

WRIGHT & PIERCE ENGINEERS   MOREHOUSE & CHESLEY ARCHITECTS

STEAMTOWN, U.S.A.

In 1962, the Governor and Council of the State of New Hampshire approved one million dollars to aid the development of a State-owned steam railroad at Keene. The great political upheaval later that year would not pass Steamtown unnoticed however, and the new administration promptly killed the proposal. Steamtown would have been the final reward of the dreams and labors of F. Nelson Blount, one of those rare patriarchs of the faithful cult of steam who has the finances, eloquence, and prestige to make a most valuable contribution to the preservation of the steam locomotive.

On his own initiative, Mr. Blount (shown here while firing for Clyde Sessions) began purchasing retired steam engines. Some were put on display at his Edaville two-foot gauge railroad at South Carver, Massachusetts. Most

20

of the engines were stored at the old B&M roundhouse at North Walpole. While acquiring his locomotives, Mr. Blount began laying plans for the elaborate facilities illustrated *above,* which included a large roundhouse, turntable, museum, station, coal tipple and a water tower.

With the Keene Chamber of Commerce drumming up enthusiasm for "Steamtown Days" among the townfolk, many of whom wore cardboard railroad caps, and radio station WKBK broadcasting live from the bright yellow coaches, the big program was launched in mid-summer of 1962. Apparently, all of this hoopla was in vain; for the skeptics who continually question Nelson Blount's motives have so disgusted him that he is ready to move his engines out of New Hampshire — for good

Meanwhile, Mr. Blount was still gathering in his locomotives from varied points of the U.S. and Canada. And what locomotives! Reading was sending its famous Northern, number 2124. A Union Pacific Big Boy was tentatively promised, as were four of the Pennsylvania's engines stored at Northumberland; bringing the 1963 total to 37 engines.

All this time, such rare locomotives as Canadian Pacific 4-4-4 No. 2929 (*above,* with a Canadian National 4-6-0) slept at the Bellows Falls enginehouse. The eventual popularity of Mr. Blount's plan is assured by five operating locomotives of Canadian origin drawing railfans from the Dominion; while the only Nickel Plate Berkshire still in steam, No. 759, built by Lima in 1944, as well as many other U.S.-built engines, promised to turn any future Steamtown into the greatest steam railroading center in North America and a dominant tourist attraction of the area in which it will be located.

In spite of petty politicians and selfish interests who will not believe a man whose honesty is beyond reproach, Nelson Blount is still hopefully seeking a home for his orphaned locomotives.

21

THE HERITAGE OF STEAM

The gauges of history by which future generations will weigh the phenomenal rise of the United States to a world power must in large part be keyed to the performance of the transportation facilities at the time of the greatest forward strides. Only when a nation is united physically can her diverse peoples feel the bonds which weld them to a common destiny and enable their energies to be channeled toward national goals in a free society.

In the memoirs of statesmen, travelers, and pioneers prior to the 1840's or '50's, are found expressions of grim frustration at the prospects of journeying the trackless forests and plains, penetrating the mountain ranges and circumventing the lakes of North America. To anyone who had suffered the rigors of a five-day stagecoach trip between Philadelphia and Pittsburgh, the thought of the hazardous journey to California must have seemed a nightmare. It is virtually impossible for a 20th century American to comprehend an economy operating with delivery schedules of weeks based on the three

miles-per-hour of the barge canal between points now only hours apart. That was the status of transport when technology reached the point where the pressing demands of rapid mass-transport were met through the means of steam and the flanged wheel on iron rails.

The brazen little locomotives of the 1830's were curiosities which evoked laughter from the haughty bargemen and carriage owners of the day. Not many years later, the humorous aspects of the iron monsters came to be tempered by the realization that the future indisputably would ride the rails. The American people coupled their destinies behind those first iron horses, and rode with them clear into the mid-20th century.

The record is clear; the railroad steam locomotive was at the heart of the evolution of the United States into a great power. As late as 1830, estimates that 200 years would elapse before the disappearance of the frontier and the consolidation of the western indian tribes were still commonly accepted in prominent national circles. But the fact was that the frontier was all but doomed less than forty years later, when the first transcontinental railroad was an accomplished fact. Where the trains went, the frontier could survive but a few years, and by 1890, when few towns were more than 200 miles from a transcontinental railway, the frontier disappeared entirely.

The impact of the railroad on the American way of life was greater than any peacetime upheaval in history. By 1840, traveling times were halved, by 1850, halved again, and so on until the whole pace of national life was determined by the railroads. The produce of all parts of the nation could be marketed in any area within a few days, and where formerly ordinary people seldom ventured more than fifty miles from home during their lifetimes, Americans took to the rails in ever increasing numbers

BALTIMORE & OHIO MUSEUM
The Baltimore & Ohio Railroad, mindful of the major role it played in the earliest years of steam railroading, has preserved the most complete collection of historical motive power of any U.S. railroad. The B&O's Transportation Museum in Baltimore, an historical railroading landmark in itself, houses this vintage equipment. Unfortunately, the necessity of economizing all levels of the Baltimore & Ohio's operations in recent years has resulted in closing the museum to the public. The twelve steam engines (including a Jersey Central Camelback and a Western Maryland Shay donated in 1954)

are all in beautiful external condition and most of them are still operable. The equipment is displayed on tracks radiating out from the turntable of the completely enclosed passenger-car roundhouse built in 1884. *Opposite,* are shown an 1890-era coach, the W. M. Shay (the last Shay built in the U.S., 1945) and the last of the Jersey Central's famous Camelbacks, a 4-4-2, No. 592. A "grasshopper" engine of 1832, the *Atlantic (above)* possessed a sophisticated technology for that early era. *Below,* the *William Mason* built in 1856, operated under its own power for Walt Disney's film version of the Great Locomotive Chase 99 years later.

bound for ever further distances.

Fortunately, many of the most important early locomotives have been preserved. They are now in museums, railroad stations, or in storage around the country. Most of them are readily accessible to the general public and several are in operating condition. Virtually all of the older preserved locomotives played a vital role in the railroad's development. On these pages are shown most of the important 19th century engines which thoughtful railroad officials began preserving even before the Civil War.

BALLOON STACKS AND BRASS POLISH

California has become a treasure house of vintage locomotives. When Nevada's Virginia & Truckee Railroad was abandoned in 1950, after using 19th Century 4-4-0's until its last years, most of its engines wound up in California. Several are owned by the motion picture industry, and two are in the Western Pacific roundhouse at Oakland, (*left*). They are the *J. W. Bowker,* a 2-4-0, and the famous *Genoa,* a 4-4-0; both Baldwin products of 1875. An even older 2-6-0 was stored outside. Along with several other engines and some rolling stock, these rare types are owned by the Pacific Coast Chapter of the Railway and Locomotive Historical Society. *Below*, the *C. P. Huntington,* a 4-2-4T, which was shipped around Cape Horn to build the Central Pacific, rests in the company of the last Southern Pacific cab-forward 4-8-8-2 near the depot in Sacramento. *opposite*, a narrow gauge Mogul named *Albert* has been beautifully restored and now operates for tourists on the Cherokee Wonderland Railroad, at Cherokee, North Carolina.

CANADIAN DISPLAYS

Although the Canadian Pacific no longer maintains records of the disposition of its steam power, quite a few CPR locomotives are known to have been earmarked for display; including one of the largest type, a 2-10-4 Selkirk, now preserved at Calgary, Alberta. The two locomotives on this page are on display at Vancouver, B. C. *Above,* No. 374, which hauled the first passenger train into that city in 1887. *Below,* the *Curly,* used in part of the original construction of the CPR, was also the first logging engine to see service in British Columbia. Now retired, it rests on a hill above Vancouver.

BREATHTAKING CLIMB

The dominant scenic attraction of the state of New Hampshire is Mount Washington, a "must" for any tour of New England. Since the 1870's a unique cog railway has carried hundreds of thousands of breathless vacationers to the summit. The same novel little locomotives which worked up the 25 per cent grade before the turn of the century still make the ten daily trips each summer. *Above,* four locomotives are visible (including a disabled one on the steep grade) and *below,* a view showing the tilted boiler of one of the four-cylinder engines, which are of unusual 0-2-2-0 wheel arrangement.

THE GENERAL

THE GREAT LOCOMOTIVE CHASE

On April 12, 1862, the most dramatic event of the War Between the States occurred. It was on this date that the "Great Locomotive Chase," also known as the Andrews Raid, was carried out almost according to plan, and came very near to shortening the War substantially. The story is now common knowledge to every school child; how a group of Union saboteurs, lead by James J. Andrews, stole the locomotive *General,* in a race against time and rainy weather to burn the wooden Chickamauga bridges and isolate General P. T. G. Beauregard and his army at Chattanooga. Since the Western & Atlantic Railroad was the main supply line between Chattanooga and Atlanta, its loss would have been catastrophic to the South. Had the raid succeeded, there would have been little chance of keeping the Union Army from invading Georgia and splitting the Confederacy by mid-1862. The Southerners pursuing the raiders recaptured the *General* intact and the engine continued in service through the war, (even acquiring a shell-hole in its stack). After many years of use, it was salvaged from a scrap line, restored and put on permanent display at Chattanooga Union Station. In 1961, the Louisville & Nashville Railroad, now owner of the W&A, reconditioned the *General* and restaged the "Chase" on the 100th anniversary of that great event.* From there, the *General* began touring the nation under steam. The oldest active

locomotive in North America, the *General* continues to acquire fame which lends almost a mystic aura to its travels. Opposite, the *General* and combine No. 665 speed from Middlesboro to Corbin, Kentucky. *Above,* the *Texas,* which finally caught the *General,* is on display in the basement of the Cyclorama Building in Atlanta. *Below,* an obviously phony *General II* now runs "locomotive chases" with an equally phony *Texas* around Georgia's scenic Stone Mountain.

---

* The *General's* story is well chronicled in the July, 1962 issue of *Trains* magazine.

MINNESOTA'S FIRST

Another famous locomotive which is preserved in a Union Station is the *William Crooks*. The first engine to operate in Minnesota, this 4-4-0 arrived at St. Paul (where it is now enshrined) by steamboat on September 9, 1861. It went to work on the St. Paul and Pacific Railroad, which is now part of the Great Northern. Also in the area of the Northwest, the Northern Pacific Railway has preserved two of its 19th century steam engines; the *Minnetonka*, used in building the original line, and an 1883 eight-wheeler. Both are in operating condition. The Great Northern and the Northern Pacific have both donated newer steam locomotives to on-line communities.

SPEED QUEENS

By the 1890's, roadbeds were sufficiently safe and motive power technology well advanced to permit phenomenal speeds on many railroads. This was the era of the "robber barons", railroad management whose business practices so infuriated the nation that they forced the creation of the monstrosity of government regulations which threatened their very existence seventy years later. Especially furious and incredibly wasteful was the rivalry of the two Eastern collossi — the New York Central and the Pennsylvania. Speed was the spirit of the waning century. The two most famous speed queens of this golden age of railroading are pictured on this page. New York Central's 999 literally astounded the world when she ran 112.5 mph in 1893, and few people believed the banner headlines. She rests on permanent display alongside a huge Santa Fe 4-8-4 at the Museum of Science and Industry in Chicago. *Below,* the great 4-4-0 as she awaited restoration in the Illinois Central yards at Homewood, Ill., in 1962. The E-2 Atlantic, No. 7002, which traveled 127.1 mph in 1905 was scrapped, but the Pennsy, with a habit for doing such things and later regretting them, resurrected an E-7 of similar appearance and refurbished it to

appear as the holder of the unbroken world's speed record.* The photo *above* was made at the P.R.R. roundhouse at Northumberland, Pennsylvania.

*The full story on both the 999 and the 7002 is contained in *Great Trains of All Time* (pp. 17-33) by Freeman Hubbard. Grosset & Dunlap, Inc. 1962.

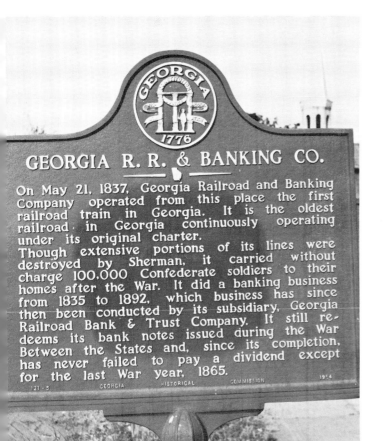

GEORGIA R. R. & BANKING CO.

On May 21, 1837, Georgia Railroad and Banking Company operated from this place the first railroad train in Georgia. It is the oldest railroad in Georgia continuously operating under its original charter.
Though extensive portions of its lines were destroyed by Sherman, it carried without charge 100,000 Confederate soldiers to their homes after the War. It did a banking business from 1835 to 1892, which business has since then been conducted by its subsidiary, Georgia Railroad Bank & Trust Company. It still redeems its bank notes issued during the War Between the States and, since its completion, has never failed to pay a dividend except for the last War year, 1865.

121-5   GEORGIA   HISTORICAL   COMMISSION   1954

STEAM IN MUSIC

When a device combined fundamental usefulness with esthetic and emotional appeal as the steam locomotive did in America, it was understandably bound to become an important factor in the cultural fabric of the nation. The haunting folk music of the Appalachians which is enjoying a revival among the young intellectuals of today, contains much in the way of railroad lyrical material. The classic "Wabash Cannonball" is but one example. The great Jimmie Rodgers, a one-time railroad engineer, imparted the synchronized beat of the steam locomotive to his music. The development of jazz was enriched by the inspiration of the steam engine. Even in 1962, two nationally popular records drew on the subject of the steam locomotive for lyrics. One was the "Blue Water Line" by the Brothers Four, which told of the plight of a fictitious little railroad of historical significance which was condemned: ". . . melt old engine number nine, and turn it into scrap." A teen-age girl began a new dance craze among the Rock'n'Roll set with

Courtesy of the Museum of Modern Art　　　　　　　　　　Gift of Mr.and Mrs. David M. Solinger.

a song based on the rhythm and movement of a steam engine. It was entitled "The Locomotion."

STEAM IN ART

So closely related were the development of the railroads and the United States that many historical markers, such as the one on the opposite page, located at Augusta, Georgia, are to be found throughout the land. The bas-relief of a steam locomotive at the upper left is among the many memorial stones in the lower recesses of the Washington Monument. Here, among the cold sculptures exhorting men of good consciencee to preserve the nation, and other stones praising the purity of the temperance movements seething in the country during the pre-Civil War era, the balloon stacked Norris engine, shamefully defiled by a century of souvenir hunters, speaks of a glory that has long faded, and a conflict which bloodied the land while forging an immortal Union. Ever since the 1830's, the steam locomotive has proven to be a versatile and adaptable subject for artists

of all schools and styles. The French Impressionists made steam and steel a vibrant thing indeed on their canvases. Right through the 1920's, when major railroads glorified their big power in calendar paintings, and the present, when artists like Howard Fogg and Otto Kuhler perpetuate the memory of steam in watercolor, the steam locomotive has been an ideal source of vibrant expressiveness. Perhaps no artist ever captured the emotions of experiencing a massive and powerful machine as did Franz Kline, (1910-1962). One of the greatest of the Abstract Expressionists, Kline often recalled his boyhood days in Pennsylvania, where the Camelbacks and coal freights influenced his artistic development. The "Chief" (*above*) is one of his most famous works, and its broad black crashing forms are very suggestive of the furious power of the steam engine. The few attempts artists have made at portraying diesels have been rather sterile, and painters have long ago forsaken the railroad yards where men like Kline and Reginald Marsh once found inspiration for their art.

33

FORLORN AND FORGOTTEN

With no hope of reprieve, hundreds of steam locomotives are rusting in despondent loneliness on weed-grown sidings, backshop tracks, and occasionally in wooded areas which long ago lost their connection with the national railroad complex.

In the last days 'of steam, when railroads of varied size were assembling their displaced engines preparatory to final dispatch to the scrap merchants, a few rusty ten-wheelers and four-coupled tank engines still managed to elude the torch. Even today, two 0-6-0's, whose Illinois Central lettering has long ago followed the rains of the seasons, stand in the grass near a Louisiana gravel pit. A Mississippi Central Mikado and a Southern Pacific switch engine still wait for the return of coal, water and a fire to rekindle the memorable yesterday of steam.

But these are forgotten dreams. A locomotive left to the dubious mercies of nature soon shows the brownish orange color of rust. If unchecked, this decay may rot through a three-quarter inch boiler wall in a few years. Long before that, however, the tubing has rotted out and all but the most massive moving parts are forever jammed with rust. Even an enthusiastic and financially solvent railfan group would probably question the feasibility of returning most of the forlorn and forgotten to any kind of service.

As the last of the steam locomotives await the inevitable scrapper's torch in their scattered retreats (some have become quite effectively camouflaged), steam fans hunt them out relentlessly. Here, then, is a photographic report of these dismal victims of "progress." Some have been decaying for twenty years, while others are only newcomers to the ranks of the locomotives in limbo. Many will remain for decades to come. Some are being cut up now.

RUSTING SADDLE-TANK ENGINES

Two of the five narrow-gauge 0-4-0T's replaced by diesels at a brickyard near Augusta, Georgia, stand behind a row of condemned dump cars.

GEORGIA RAILROAD ROUNDHOUSE

Many old steam servicing areas still survive. Such a place is the Georgia Railroad roundhouse in Augusta. Bad-order boxcars now populate stalls once claimed by Pacifics and 4-6-0's. In the guise of an old axle lathe, a huge press, and racks of boiler tubing (*right*), the ghost of steam will haunt the old building until it is finally razed to make way for facilities of a less picturesque nature.

SUNSET ON THE KANAWHA

The locomotive builders' art reached near perfection during the 1930's and '40's with construction of several hundred 2-8-4 Berkshires for five eastern roads. Essentially cousins in looks and performance, the Lima 2-8-4's of the Pere Marquette, the Nickel Plate and the Erie and the Lima and American Locomotive Company's Kanawhas which hauled coal over the Appalachians for the Chesapeake & Ohio and the Virginian, were just what the builders and the satisfied railroads expected—and more. Big and powerful, these 2-8-4's were the queens of the "super-power" era. The 90

C & O 2-8-4's were perhaps the greatest of the truly great. Held in such high esteeem by the railroad, there are, fortunately, quite a few preserved Kanawhas — including one in glistening grandeur and perfect running condition at the National Railroad Museum, Green Bay, Wisconsin. In late Summer of 1962, four of these wonderful engines, clothed in a macabre mantle of time and rust, still occupied a track behind the diesel shops at Russell, Kentucky. In deference to the modesty of a magnificent lady, we see here Kanawha No. 2756, her aging minimized in silhouette, before her final sunset.

36

THE GREAT ALLEGHENY

If any latter day steam locomotives conjured visions of "what might have been," it was Chesapeake & Ohio's sixty great 2-6-6-6 Allegheny types built by Lima between 1941 and 1948. Big, powerful, beautiful — the Allegheny was all of these — as well as the latest type of articulated engine to see regular service. The 2-6-6-6 suggested the possibility of a 4-8-6 and perhaps even a 4-10-6. The diesel never gave these ideas a chance, but that six-wheel trailing truck was a ponderable thing, indeed. The Allegheny *above* is kept company by the 4-8-4 Greenbriar behind it, a 2-8-2 and the aforementioned Kanawhas at Russell Yard.

BIG ALICE

Once they called her "the goon." The Chicago, Burlington and Quincy owned but thirteen Hudsons. Twelve of them were constructed by Baldwin in 1930. Seven years later, Hudson No. 3002 was renumbered 4000, and covered with one of those tasteless shrouds which so many railroads seemed to feel "beautified" steam locomotives during the pre-World War II streamlining craze. The engine was named *Aeolus* (the keeper of the winds), but irreverent observers preferred "Big Alice, the Goon." War-time restrictions removed the shroud in 1941. "Big Alice" was the last Hudson on Burlington property, *below,* at Galesburg, Illinois.

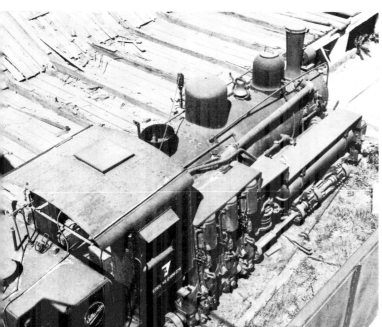

LAST OF MISSABE STEAM

Articulateds of the Duluth, Missabe and Iron Range still pulled railfan trips in the early sixties. In 1962, several "last steam runs" on the Missabe were run by fan groups behind 2-10-2's (*upper left, above photo*). Then it seemed Missabe would drop the fires for the last time. Here, at Proctor, Minnesota, mammoth grey-jacketed Yellowstones and Santa Fe types are spending their last days in the sun. The four huge tenders — ironically still loaded with coal — parked next to a line-up of 2-8-8-4's, have already lost the Yellowstones they once trailed. At *left*, a three truck Willamette Shay of the Medford Corporation in Oregon rests outside the lumber mill where she once worked.

FUGITIVES FROM THE TORCH

There are, at various locations around the United States, places where a scrapper's torch is a seemingly unknown instrument. Witness the two locomotives on this page. *Above,* a Marianna & Blountstown ten-wheeler built in 1911 (souvenir hunters had not yet absconded with her Baldwin builder's plate) allows young trees to grow about her disintegrating pilot beam during a Florida December twilight. It would be difficult to estimate when the 4-6-0 last waddled over to Marianna; probably not since World War II. In the finest short-line tradition of saving everything, the little locomotive remains outside the enginehouse at Blountstown, while M&B's diesel growls about its daily business. Already minus such decorative appurtenances as stack, bell, pilot coupler and headlight, the old engine gives the appearance of returning to the earth from whence she came. The 0-6-0 of unknown origin, *below,* has found its last resting place on the sands but a short distance from Lake Ontario, in upper New York State.

Modern Union Pacific steam power always was a matter of superlatives. U.P. pioneered both the 4-6-6-4 Challenger and 4-8-8-4 Big Boy simple articulated types. The locomotive with the largest rigid driver wheelbase in the United States was the 9000 series 4-12-2 type, named for the Union Pacific which originated it. Even four years after total dieselization (Big Boys last hauled revenue freight in July 1959), trackside townspeople on the U.P. still recall with admiration, the magic number "800" in reference to the sleek 4-8-4's of which few survive; two on the scrap line at Cheyenne.

Of all the locomotives Union Pacific dispatched across the continental divide, none could compare with the greatest of all steam power: twenty-five engines, numbered 4000-4024 and known to Union Pacific men simply as "four thousands." These were the Big Boys. With tenders they weighed over 1,250,000 pounds and could consume 22 tons of coal an hour when working a freight drag up Wyoming's Sherman Hill. Measuring 132 feet from pilot to rear of tender, the Big Boys were the longest steam locomotives in the world, and the only 4-8-8-4's ever built. It wasn't until 1961,

SCRAPPING A BIG BOY

Left, the front engine of No. 4021 is being cut up in the foreground, while the boiler, completely stripped, rests on timbers. *Right,* a shop worker cutting inside the firebox, sends out cascades of molten steel. A few more days, and 4021 was gone.

when Union Pacific was sure its diesels could safely handle all peak traffic loads, that the Big Boys could be disposed of. Even then, retirement of these fantastic machines was slow and cautious. By September 1962, three had been donated for permanent exhibit, four were still in operational condition at Green River, Wyoming, seven were on the scrap line at Cheyenne and two others were on the property — one was to have been sent to Argentina. When the recipients in that country could not raise the money to ship the engine, she was left at Green River. The nine other Big Boys have been scrapped.

On these pages, 4-8-8-4, No. 4021 is being cut up, while outside the huge engine shops at Cheyenne, other 4000's await the end with Nos. 833 and 836. Sister 844 (recently renumbered 8444) is U.P.'s last active steamer, and sometimes runs as far as Ogden, Utah, with fantrip specials.

While Union Pacific has been procrastinating in the final disposition of its 4000's, the scrapping of all of its other steam power has been about equal in rapidity to most other railroads. All but one each of the 88 4-12-2's and the 115 2-10-2's have been scrapped. U.P. owned 105 Challengers — more than any other road — but probably not a half dozen were left at the end of 1962. At a far corner of the Cheyenne yard, a pathetic and silent last double-header was maintained by a Big Boy and a Challenger. Behind them were at least thirty tenders — all that remained of the 3700 and 3800 series 4-6-6-4's.

The Union Pacific has donated many 2-8-0's, 0-6-0's and other comparatively small types to towns and museums, and in 1962, 4-8-4 No. 814 was put on display at Council Bluffs, Iowa.

BIG BOYS AT BAY

Below, the last 2-10-2 on Union Pacific property, No. 5511, casts a homely glance forward, while a 4000 stands in dismal silence in one of the extended stalls especially constructed for the Big Boys at Green River. It was this engine, number 4005, which had been partially dismantled for shipment to Argentina. The tenders of four other 4-8-8-4's are visible from the turntable (*above*). 4009 and 4010 were condemned and would be towed to Cheyenne for scrapping.

TWO FOR POSTERITY

On the *opposite* page is a reality to gratify all friends of steam. Far-sighted Union Pacific, well aware of the debt it owes to its celebrated steam powered engines, recently completely overhauled a late-model Challenger and the second newest Big Boy. Resplendent in shining rods and fresh paint, these giants occupy two stalls in cathedral-like magnificence at Cheyenne roundhouse. They are in perfect running condition, and the discerning Union Pacific plans to keep them indefinitely.

The wood of the shovel is gray and cracked. Rust has long since covered the twisted fire iron. Last Autumn's leaves lie scattered over the coal pile worn down by the rains of many seasons. The old Consolidation's boiler jacket, ruptured at the bottom, has spilled white asbestos lagging onto the decaying ties. Lonely-looking and with a dismal future, No. 223 waits for the scrapper's torch in East Dublin, Georgia. The fuel that was to make the great heat of power never will reach her firebox; for the coal and steel of the steam age are no more today than masts and sails were yesterday, or oil and aluminum will be tomorrow. Technology leaves the past great in its wake — and memories. Memories of November 1907, when Baldwin built the little Consolidation. Of the days when she was the pride of the forty-mile Wrightsville and Tennille Railroad. Of a hot fire.

The picture was made on Christmas Eve. A mile away, a diesel was switching near Dublin station. Who remembers No. 223 in the days since her economic usefulness has waned?

HER LAST DAYS

2-8-0 No. 223 of the Wrightsville & Tennille Railroad faces a dubious future behind a weathered coal pile which in all probability will never pass through her cold firebox doors.

45

Left, the last of 2,033 H-6 Consolidations peers out of its stall at the Northumberland roundhouse.

the Pennsylvania. A brief look at statistics defines the term "total dieselization" in terribly clear terms to the steam fan at Northumberland. The Pennsylvania had 301 locomotives of the 4-8-2 type — the famous M-1. No. 6755 is the only one remaining. Standing in cold sobriety next to the M-1 is the last of the fat Decapods which once waddled all over the Keystone system. Of 598 I-1 2-10-0's the Pennsy once boasted, No. 4483 is the only one remaining. Her many sisters, all built between 1916 and 1923, have long been gone; leaving the persistent 4483 to ponder her good fortune.

Huddled together are three smaller but equally renowned examples of the Pennsylvania's successful experience with standardization. 0-6-0 No. 1670 is the only one of 312 B-6's in existence. One of the 121 G-5 4-6-0's built in the mid-twenties for both the P.R.R. and the L.I.R.R., occupies the track next to No. 460, the most-famous E-6 Atlantic. The 83 E-6's were the predecessors of the greatest of all of the P.R.R.'s motive power — the K-4 Pacific. No. 460 gained fame through her 100-mph runs between Philadelphia and New York during the 1920's.

SLUMBERING AT NORTHUMBERLAND

During World War II, the vast trackage of the mighty Pennsylvania Railroad throbbed to the tremendous vociferation of over 4,500 steam locomotives. In December 1957, a few I-1 Decapods still assigned to coal drags were dispossessed by the now ubiquitous diesels and the great belpaire-boilered engines passed on to oblivion. The Pennsy, however, was not soon to forget the distinguished engines spawned at Juniata and quietly saved one of each of their most numerous types at the sleepy little town of Northumberland.

Priceless treasure is secreted beyond the roundhouse doors. Here nine engines, oblivious of the pigeons which populate the roundhouse, or the occasional melancholy railfans who come to reminisce, wait out the long seasons. Adjacent to the roundhouse are five more engines. Each of these is the last survivor of its type on

LONG-DISTANCE TENDERS

Huge tenders of M-1 Mountains were fifty-two feet long; only three feet less than locomotive.

LAST OF THE BELPAIRE SPECIES

Above: 0-6-0, 4-6-0 and 4-4-2 stand on tracks radiating out from the turntable. These engines have been parked here for years; will need major repairs before being put on display. The sloped back was typical among switch engine tenders, for visibility is important in yard operations, as is the bright back-up light for night operations.

DESTINED FOR DISPLAY

Below: Lined up front to rear, are an M-1, I-1, B-6, G-5 and E-6. For years the Pennsylvania has hoped to donate these locomotives to museums, but could never afford to repair and restore them. Recently some steps were being taken in this direction, however, with word from the Pennsy that a K-4 was being renovated in the road's shops.

THE SAD END OF THE LOUISIANA EASTERN

An article in the June 1962, issue of *Railroad Magazine* asked anxiously: "What will happen to the Louisiana Eastern?" The answer was all too apparent by September. Here, beyond a veritable mountain of driving wheel tires at a Louisiana gravel pit, three locomotives were being butchered while No. 11, a Mikado which in recent years had become quite a prima donna, awaited her turn.

Paulson Spence was a great admirer of the steam locomotive and fortunately possessed both the desire and the substance to acquire thirty of them before he died in 1961. Mr. Spence used his steam power to move gravel over his Louisiana Eastern shortline and to keep the numerous railfans who visited his domain in complete ecstasy. His big plans to keep most of his engines running are apparent from the stockpiles of feedwater heaters, engine tires, grates, airpumps, and heavy machinery on the property. Since his death, railfans have deplored the fact that no one stepped forward to save his beloved locomotives. They feel his heirs could at least have been slower to destroy them.

GREAT NORTHERN'S LAST

The Great Northern Railway gathered in the last of its steam engines in the 1960's for final disposition to the torch. A 4-8-2, No. 2510, (*left*) lacking much, including her tender, spent her waning days outside the roundhouse at Superior, Wisconsin. A discarded tender and flocks of pigeons were her only comfort, as road diesels prowled the tracks nearby. A mile away, the remaining Great Northern steam power occupied two long tracks. Once assembled, these most modern of G.N. steam engines, their piston rods severed, were to be towed to a scrap yard. Included in the rusty line-up were big belpaire-firebox 2-8-8-0's and 2-8-8-2's, 4-8-2's, 2-8-2's and 4-8-4's. Meanwhile, a midwestern fan group was working hard to save one of G.N.'s last 4-8-4's, to "get up steam once more."

SHAY LOGGERS

The huge diesel trucks have rolled through the Pacific Northwest, sweeping clear the logging railroads before their onslaught. By 1961, all but a few of these little railroads were forsaken. Virtually all those remaining had acquired diesel locomotives. Then West Side Lumber Company near Tuolumne, California, abandoned the last steam-powered narrow-gauge logging road in the United States and left its seven remaining Shays in the yard (*below*). A standard gauge Heisler was still switching around the mill when a protracted strike shut down operations in April 1962. There was then some speculation that a portion of the line might be sold for a fan enterprise, along with several of the engines. The memory of these rustic little railroads deserves such a respectful perpetuation.

LATTER-DAY CLINCHFIELD ARTICULATEDS

Shrouded by nearly a decade of rust, a line of huge articulateds becomes ever more entwined with wet weeds in the yard of the condemned at Erwin, Tennessee. Here is where the Clinchfield Railroad gathers its bad-order hoppers and gondolas. Here too, the mighty engines wait for the oblivion of time to pass into the brief pain of the acetylene torch, when they will be forever gone.

These big simple 4-6-6-4's are indicative of the waste spawned by the rush to dieselize. Built by American Locomotive Works at a cost of over $305,000 each in 1947, they saw only six years of service; then were "stored" at Erwin. Their scrap value is approximately $20,000 per engine. It would cost twice that to restore them to service. The big Challengers need cherish no illusions of a return to the coal drags of yesterday, however, for they have already been consigned to scrap.

RUSTING IN CAROLINA

One of the most interesting graveyards of the forlorn and forgotten was to be found until the early '60's in the small town of Sanford, North Carolina. In the yard of the Atlantic & Western Railroad, two Consolidations, their boiler jackets penetrated with thick vines right up to their cab roofs, decayed in the company of a ramshackle gasoline car. On the following pages are the engines as they looked from the l.c.l. section of the car. In the *right background,* across the turntable pit, the cylinder saddle of a scrapped ten-wheeler may still be seen. Wheels and other parts of destroyed engines littered the area, and nearby, two elderly workmen were dismantling the A & W's venerable caboose.

51

THE LAST OF CANADIAN STEAM POWER

The steam locomotive meant more to the development and civilizing of Canada than perhaps any other nation, including the United States. The Canadian Pacific literally united Canada at a time when there was an imminent break between the eastern provinces and the west. The diamond-stacked engines which twenty years before had created an eternal bond between Atlantic and Pacific across the U.S. did likewise for Canada.

After World War I, the many bankrupt roads of Canada merged into the government-owned Canadian National Railways. The giant Canadian Pacific remained in private ownership and is the only sizable railroad outside of the United States not government-controlled. The great era of steam in Canada saw two huge systems — the C N R and the C P R — with their distinctive trends in motive power. While C N R owned over 200 Northerns, C P R built only two experimentals. Canadian Pacific hung cylindrical shrouds over virtually everything, while the Canadian National found itself in possession of a heterogeneous conglomeration of locomotives from the roundhouses of railroads it had absorbed.

The schedule of dieselization reached the climax in Canada only two or three years after most U.S. roads had banished the steam loco-

motive. In 1963 only one steam engine, Canadian National 4-8-4 No. 6167, was available for fan trips. There were a few industrial and shortline engines left, but for all practical purposes, steam is deader in the Dominion than it probably ever will be in the United States. All Canadian National locomotives have been disposed of except three old engines which are part of C N R's museum train and a few others still on the property awaiting final disposition. As of 1962, fifty other engines had been donated or sold. At least seventeen of these locomotives are owned by United States citizens; most of them are or will be operating in the U.S. Probably the most famous C N R survivor is the Strasburg Rail Road's charming little 0-6-0 in Pennsylvania. The Railroad Club of Chicago occasionally runs a 4-6-2 from CNR's subsidiary, Grand Trunk, and Nelson Blount planned to bring no less than nine Canadian engines to his projected "Steamtown" in New Hampshire. Fortunately, there are several examples of virtually every Canadian National type in existence, from the personable and immensely amiable little Moguls and 4-6-0's which until so recently trundled the barren branchlines, up to the big 4-8-4's and 2-10-2's of the high iron. They are on display at various points throughout the Dominion.

CANADIAN CONGLOMERATION

Near the huge Point St. Charles shops in Montreal (*left*) one of the last gatherings of Canadian steam awaits the completion of the Canadian Railroad Historical Association's museum at Delson, Quebec. These ten locomotives of eight different wheel arrangements are as indicative of CNR steam power as may be found in one collection. The 4-6-4T, No. 49, one of the last suburban tank engines to operate in North America, was the last steam locomotive overhauled at Point St. Charles.

ONCE BUSY ROUNDHOUSE

Of all the structures involved in railroading, none held such fascination as the roundhouse. Like the steam locomotives they once sheltered, roundhouses are rapidly disappearing. The fifty-six stalls of Canadian National's Turcot roundhouse once resounded to the labors of over 950 workers and the moving of 100 locomotives every 24 hours. The wreckers ended the 57 year saga of North America's largest roundhouse in 1962, when its function was taken over by the new Montreal yard.

THEY FOUGHT STEAM'S LAST BATTLE

The three 4-6-2's (*below*) which lay idle at the edge of the Canadian Pacific yards near Montreal were the only steam locomotives left on that road's property. Nos. 1227 and 1270 in the company of G3g, No. 2409, were the last of 102 light Pacifics built between 1944 and 1948 especially for branch-line service. They were wonderful efficient little engines which hinted at revolutionizing operations in areas of light traffic by replacing old downgraded road engines. These valiant locomotives fought steam's last great battle against the encroachments of the diesel which rose up out of the south to impose monotony upon the once beautiful motive power rosters of Canada.

MONUMENTS AND MUSEUMS

It was only when steam power began to disappear rapidly in the latter '40's, that the railroads answered the pleas of railfans who had long advocated saving representative examples of all locomotive types of the steam era.

American railroads, with a few painfully notable exceptions (for example, New York Central), answered the exhortations of the historically-minded and the steam buffs with nearly 500 locomotives — mostly donated — set aside for "preservation." The Santa Fe has given forty-five steam engines to on-line communities and museums, including quite a few of their monster 4-8-4's and 2-10-4's. For a time, it seemed that more of Chesapeake and Ohio's famed Kanawhas would wind up in parks than in scrap yards. Three of Union Pacific's Big Boys were museum pieces in 1963, with negotiations under way for several more; including the 4012, which was to go to Steamtown, New Hampshire, 1500 miles from the nearest U.P. rails.

There are, at various parks and Legion Halls, tanks and artillery pieces saved as trophies of great conflicts. Occasionally, an old fire engine may be left at a playground for children to clamber upon. Never, however, among all the machines of peace and war, has a society elected to save so many examples of an "obsolete" contrivance as have Americans in the preservation of their beloved steam locomotives. The steam engine stands alone among all the creations of man with the distinction of having hundreds of monuments — "dedicated to the vanishing Age of Steam" or "in memory of the steam locomotive" — erected to eulogize its passing.

Upon reflection, it may be noted that when the luxurious Boeing Stratocruiser was retired

FLOPHOUSE ON RAILS

The huge flat top of a Southern Pacific articulated's tender is "home" to several tramps in Sacramento, California, and their personal effects lie scattered about, sheltered from weather and public view by overhanging tree boughs. Liquor bottles, filthy blankets and obscene novels are hardly fitting tributes to the memory of the great fleet of fine articulated steam locomotives once maintained by the Espee. A fence would put a stop to such desecration, and return the dignity due this engine.

VANDALIZED PACIFIC

Pacific No. 470 was a classic example of her type, and the last steam locomotive to operate over the tracks of the Maine Central. The day of her retirement, in June 1954, was one of remembrance for much of Maine as the beautiful 4-6-2, paced by television cameras, newsmen and radio trucks, ran over much of the southern portion of the state. Now on permanent exhibit at Waterville, No. 470 is obviously only appreciated by the town vandals. She has been repainted, but a fence is needed.

by the airlines, no "fan groups" chartered any of these aircraft for a "last ride" or a "journey to the past." Someone has yet to publish a roster of North American Van Line's motive power and equipment, let alone to market it for twelve dollars a copy. And who would stand shivering for hours at the edge of Route 66 in December to get a "sunrise shot" of a Trailways bus? Yet all these affections of mankind are lavished upon the steam locomotive.

Unfortunately, the generosity of the railroads was too often taken for granted by the recipients of the mammoth gifts and soon after the elaborate dedication ceremonies — usually attended by railroad, town and even state officials — the "last steam locomotive to arrive at Podunk" was rusting unattended, vandalized and stripped of everything not welded down. There were too many Podunks; and their story is, sadly enough, woven all through the last days of steam. Several detailed examples of this shame appear on these pages. Usually, the simple act of erecting a fence topped with barbed wire is sufficient to deter vandals. If a locomotive is in a more secluded place, a few lamp posts may also help. Certainly, if the railroads are willing to donate engines worth thousands of dollars as scrap and if the unions give hours without pay to installing them in exhibit areas, the recipients have the responsibility of maintaining them in presentable condition. Most of the engines that the Sante Fe scattered around eastern Kansas are now in deplorable condition. Perhaps it would have been far wiser to scrap thirty-five or forty of those donated engines and have kept five or ten of them in running condition for fan trips, where they would have been appreciated rather than desecrated.

"TWO HUNDRED TONS OF JUNK"

This is the term applied to locomotives such as the once-formidable Nickel Plate Mikado (*right*), by M. H. Klebolt, president of the Illini Railroad Club and an advocate of more operating steam engines and less rotting airpump jackets, smashed headlights and peeling paint. Mr. Klebolt also feels that a few preserved engines indoors or on museum grounds where they are protected, are preferable to hundreds of them left to the fate being endured by No. 624, at Hammond, Indiana. After seeing scores of such locomotives (their numbers outweighing the well maintained ones), the author cannot help but agree with Mr. Klebolt's strongly expressed views on steam engine preservation.

MEXICAN DISPLAY

Across the street from the ultra-modern Buena-vista Station in Mexico City, a quaint little 0-4-2T shop engine of European build has been placed on permanent display. There are still a few British switchers to be seen on the property of the National Railways of Mexico, including a Kitson 0-6-0T (1904) in the Valle de Mexico round-house. Although unfenced and resting on an ample supply of stone ballast, the immaculate locomotive shows no signs of vandalism — a fact which may give pause to visiting United States railfans. Many Mexicans share the enthusiasm for steam power felt by their northern neighbors.

GRIFFITH PARK LOCOMOTIVES

Griffith Park, in Los Angeles, has sixteen loco-motives on display, along with some rolling stock and trolley cars. *Above:* Until recently, this nar-row-gauge 4-6-0 of the Oahu Railway and Land Company transported children around the park. Overhauling her would be too costly, so the South-ern Pacific narrow gauge equipment and the coaches which carried plantation workers in Hawaii have become inactive and are likely to remain so.

ARTICULATING ARTICULATED

The last surviving Norfolk & Western Y-6 articu-lated, No. 2156, is now on display at the Museum of Transport, near St. Louis. These engines were built in N & W's own shops as late as 1952, and some were only eight years old when scrapped!

BACKWARD ARTICULATEDS

In all the annals of steam, few locomotives were equal to Southern Pacific's fantastic AC (articulated-consolidation) cab-forward locomotives in performance and fame (*below*). Before the steam age crumbled after the Second World War, Espee had acquired no less than 256 "backward" articulateds of three different wheel arrangements. It all began in 1928 when the S.P. ordered a 2-8-8-2 turned around to enable the crew to ride ahead of the exhaust which on previous Mallets had practically asphyxiated enginemen in the long Sierra tunnels and snowsheds. Eventually 195 of the renowned 4100 and 4200 series locomotives handled passengers and freight with equal facility. (They were the only 4-8-8-2's ever built; but if one considers the smokebox truck first and the firebox truck last, they were actually Yellowstones). All the cab-forwards were, quite naturally, oil burners. Considering the great success and unsurpassed visibility of these locomotives, it seems strange that no other railroad adopted the cab-forward principle. The sole survivor of this magnificent breed of articulateds is number 4294, a Baldwin graduate of 1944, now on display at the Sacramento station. She was also the last new steam locomotive purchased by the Southern Pacific.

TEXAS NOCTURNE

She was beautiful in an unesthetic manner. She was a big freight engine which revolutionized the motive-power thinking of the '20's. She was as her name implied; huge, magnificent and proud. This was the original 2-10-4 Texas type — one of the most important locomotives ever built. The Texas & Pacific ordered seventy engines of the 600 series in 1925-28 and ended the drag freight era for good. The Texas types could haul nearly 50% more weight at an increase of one-third over the speed of the 2-10-2's they replaced. These engines probably did more to update the T & P's operational thinking than the latter day diesels of dubious advantage. So revered were these locomotives that when the first batch was retired in 1949,

many Texans clamored for their preservation. So it was that the "world's largest Christmas gift"— 2-10-4 No. 638, wrapped from smokebox to tender back in a huge red ribbon, was given to the city of Dallas. Then followed the most infamous scandal in the preservation of locomotives. Vandals damaged the 638 so badly that the T & P disgustedly cut her up on the spot. No. 610, the only remaining Texas, is now kept in near-immaculate condition at Fort Worth's Will Rogers Park. A tall cyclone fence. crowned with barbed wire, and a nearby lamp post, assure the 610 its properly remembered role as the venerated sire of the 2-10-4 wheel arrangement — which eventually was adopted by over a dozen other railroads.

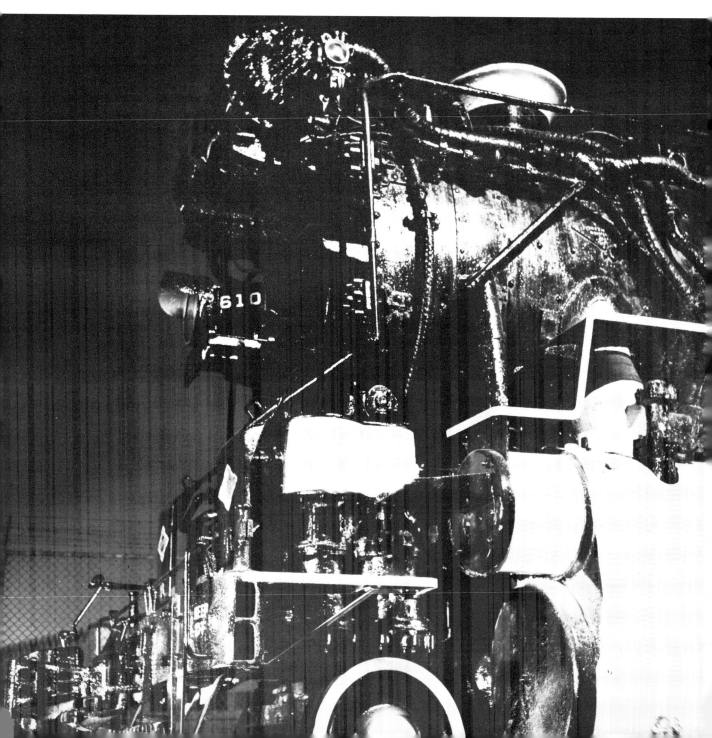

ESPEE IN SAN ANTONIO

The city of San Antonio, being quite historically minded as the early place of Texas independence and the location of the heroic Alamo, quite naturally agrees that the Mikado which the Southern Pacific has seen fit to donate be well cared for. Until midnight, all her lamps, including the cab and tender lights, are illuminated, and her running gear is spot lighted. After operating out of San Antonio for forty years, the 2-8-2 was placed on display in 1957.

THE LAST OF LONG ISLAND STEAM

Gone are the E-6's which wheeled the fishing specials to Montauk. Gone too, are the K-4's which ran the mainline through Suffolk farmlands and scrub pine to Riverhead and Greenport. All of the chunky H-10 Consolidations which worked the branchlines and factory sidings of Nassau County have disappeared. Standing in the solitary aplomb that is the lot of all monuments to greater things in more glorious times, one of the two surviving Long Island Rail Road steam locomotives — both G-5 4-6-0's — rests in perpetual retirement at Nassau's Salisbury Park. *Left*, an indulgent parent attempts to inform the diesel generation of the soot and fury that was the run to Huntington, to Smithtown and Port Jefferson, where this pigeon-defiled ten wheeler, along with No. 38, preserved at the Carriage Museum in Stonybrook, performed most of her tasks. At the time of dieselization on the Long Island Rail Road, all of its steam power had been built by the Pennsylvania, which controlled it until shortly after the disastrous trio of wrecks in 1950. However, during the early existence of the Long Island (dating back to 1834), it had a wide variety of individualistic motive power types, including Camelbacks and tank engines. The Pennsy standardized the L.I.R.R.'s steam power with H-6 and H-10 Consolidations, some K-4's and E-6's, as well as 0-8-0 and 0-6-0 yard "goats." The thirty-one G-5's were perhaps the heaviest 4-6-0's ever built and the most modern designed in the United States. Pennsy built them for the L.I.R.R. during the '20's especially for the rapid-acceleration commuter service.

THE GREATEST OF 4-6-2's

One of the most successful locomotives produced by an American railroad was the Pennsylvania's great K-4 Pacific, 425 of which were built between 1914 and 1927. An indication of the great respect the Pennsy had for this locomotive is the fact that one of her type was selected as the railroad's monument to its steampower at the famous Horseshoe Curve, near Altoona. At *left,* K-4 No. 1361, just a few feet from the high iron which once saw so much action in steam and was a virtual Mecca for rail photographers, silently broods over a passing diesel-powered coal drag on a rainy June day. Few people visit Horseshoe Curve today, since the big show of steam has vanished. The K-4 *below,* renumbered 1737, bears the keystone plate of the first of her type, which was scrapped long ago. For years she has been stored in the roundhouse at Northumberland, awaiting renovation. Both surviving K-4's have the high headlights and solid pilots of the late '40's; not typical of their class.

BEST OF THE SOUTH AND THE WEST

One of the few beautiful streamlined engines was the Southern Pacific's famous GS series 4-8-4's, 60 of which were built. The simple secret of their appeal was that rather than trying to hide the locomotive under an applied shroud, Lima built these engines with a conservative amount of streamlining which was part of the original conception. The flaring smokebox door, solid pilot and skyline casing tended to accentuate the locomotive rather than hide it. When these engines, painted red, orange, black and white, wheeled the legendary orange Daylights through the Pacific coast mountains, Californians declared them the "world's most beautiful trains." They were. No. 4460 (*at left*), the last GS, is at the Museum of Transport, in St. Louis. *Below:* The last of the Southern Railway's legendary green and gold PS-4 Pacifics will be on perpetual display in the new Transportation Building of the Smithsonian Institution in Washington, D. C. Completely rehabilitated by the Southern, including sand blasting and paint mixed according to the original formula, this locomotive is the ideal example of how an engine should be preserved. At night she will be floodlighted, and passing motorists will be able to view her through a 110-foot long plate glass window. The tarpaulin protects the 4-6-2 until the building is completed.

IRONIC "PRESERVATION"

We have seen that the steam locomotives placed on display throughout the land by accommodating railroads have come to varied ends — many quite unfortunate. On the facing page, the top photo shows Maine Central's last Pacific, No. 470, as she stands today in Waterville. The beautiful engine is far removed indeed from June 13, 1954, when thousands lined the right-of-way and station platforms to pay silent respect to her last run. Philip R. Hastings did an admirable job of capturing 470's last hours for the September 1954 issue of *Trains,* and when one compares those pictures with the locomotive today, it may well be argued that the torch would have been a more honorable fate. Of all the scandalous "preservation" debacles, the two 0-6-0's — one Southern Pacific, the other Union Pacific — at *left,* are the most ironic. Like most locomotives on display within a few hundred miles of Promontory, these hapless 20th Century switchers at Ogden, Utah, are coupled pilot to pilot in some esoteric symbolism supposedly representing the golden spike ceremony. The plaque in the foreground reads: "The people of Ogden and Weber County have placed these locomotives as a memorial in grateful acknowledgement of the contributions to our region by the railroad industry and the railroad men and women since the driving of the golden spike, May 10, 1869." This whole affair was erected in 1959 by various reputable local civic groups. The engines are in a deplorable state, smashed and rusting, with missing parts and cabs which now see frequent service as latrines. This is an affront to the railroads and a wry comment upon the "grateful" people of Ogden.

GEORGIAN MIKADO

Above: The only survivor of a magnificent lineage of high-stacked Pacifics and trim Mikados, Georgia Railroad's 302 stands behind the new Augusta court house. The railroad's classic ten-wheelers so typical of the Georgian beauty which graced motive power rosters of the deep South, have also gone before the torch. No. 302 is showing the first signs of decay in this picture. When it was taken, a group of townspeople was contemplating a sheltering roof for the graphite-faced Mike.

KENTUCKY RAILWAY MUSEUM

Below: The Kentucky Railway Museum in Louisville, is an expanding organization possessing a C & O Kenawha, an L & N Pacific and a small Vulcan tank engine, as well as some fine rolling stock, including the "Jim Crow" combine which the celebrated *General* is currently hauling around the nation. L & N No. 152 is probably the oldest 4-6-2 in existence as is evident in the fact that her trailing axle is rigid. She resembles an Atlantic with an additional axle, more than a true Pacific.

TWENTY MILES APART

Some towns take pride in the locomotives railroads have donated. Others leave their engines to nature and vandals. Pacific No. 107 came to the Georgia Northern from the Florida East Coast Railroad, where it had run for years as No. 88. American built the once dapper 4-6-2 in 1911. Now she rots away on the edge of a park playground in Albany, Georgia. Twenty miles from Albany, in the small village of Sylvester, a monument to steam has been built with a fine little Mikado. She once belonged to a small south Georgia line with the impressive title of Georgia, Ashburn, Sylvester & Camilla Railroad. The 2-8-2, built by Baldwin in 1930, now sports a fresh coat of paint and a corrugated metal roof. The roof supports annoy photographers, but more important, the roof protects the locomotive from weather and the barbed wire keeps vandals away.

OPERATING RAILWAY MUSEUMS

Perhaps one-third of the operating steam locomotives in the United States are owned by railroad museums. Most of these ambitious projects began in a small way; perhaps by a fan group purchasing a few hundred feet of abandoned track, or one railfan spending two hundred dollars for an old wood caboose. From such a simple start, eventually the attractive possibility of acquiring an engine may present itself. If the group is equal to the task (and fortunately, most of them are) it may soon spend its Sunday afternoons firing up and running its own locomotive. As the news spreads, the "operating museum" becomes a local, then a national, attraction. The Ohio Railway Museum is such a success story. From humble beginnings in 1948, it now owns two steam locomotives in top running shape plus a large roster of traction equipment from trolley cars to maintenance-of-way and freight units — all in various stages of service and several being renovated at one time. A refrigerator car serves as a tool house and a railroad bookstore helps defray expenses. At *left,* the last operational Norfolk & Western steamer, 4-6-2 No. 578, chuffs down the right of way which once belonged to the Columbus, Delaware and Marion Electric Railroad, at Worthington,

Ohio. *Above:* On the grounds of the Iron Horse Motel at Golden, the Colorado Railroad Museum contains the most complete collection of narrow gauge railroad equipment, documents, posters, tickets, etc. in existence. Guests at the motel are admitted free, and other visitors pay a nominal fee to browse among fascinating photographs and old headlights and to climb about the equipment. The museum, located on route 58, is open all year, and when the cat is not digging around the stub switch, Rio Grande Consolidation No. 346 may be seen puttering around the yard if a special occasion, such as a visiting railfan group, warrants it. The former Florence and Cripple Creek No. 318 may soon be made operational as well. The famous Rio Grande Southern 4-6-0, No. 20, is also on the property, along with a considerable amount of rolling stock and plenty of rails and switches. The museum also publishes a paper, quite informative on the doings of contemporary steam around the U.S., known as the "Iron Horse News." *Right:* A huge Baldwin 4-10-2 experimental engine of the 1920's, and the 60,000th locomotive built by that company, "operates" in an unusual manner. On display inside Philadelphia's Franklin Institute, the engine is moved a few feet each hour by an electric motor; hardly equal to her glorious past.

LIVE STEAM PRESERVED FOR FANS

During the early 1960's, the active steam locomotive population in New York State was on the rise. In 1962, the Arcade and Attica, a shortline at the western end of the state, placed an ex-Boyne City (Michigan) Consolidation in service hauling weekend picnickers. Then a rehabilitated 2-6-2 was put in operation by the Empire State Railway Museum at Middletown. The little two foot gauge engines which the proprietors of Freedomland in New York City have rented from the Edaville Railroad are one of the park's most popular attractions. One of these operations is Rail City, near Sandy Creek, on the edge of Lake Ontario. The motive power is the large Mogul, No. 11, of the Bath and Hammondsport, shown at *left*. The B & H is known as "The Champagne Route" in deference to its main reason for a long and bubbly existence; to start vintage Champagne from Hammondsport, New York, one of the largest producers of the beverage, to the national markets. Now the Mogul hauls tourists during the Summer months, and she looks much the same as when she was in revenue service. Her engineer, Chauncey S. Covey, a fascinating old-timer of 75, is also the fireman and master mechanic. Recently this venerable railroader overhauled No. 11 virtually single-handedly! Mr. Covey began his railroad career by firing on the New York Central in 1906. There is also quite a bit of other rolling stock on the grounds, including a Huntingdon and Broad Top Mountain 2-8-0 and a dozen 0-4-0T's. Another new operation (*lower left*) is the Indiana Museum of Transport & Communication, Inc. which, like many shortlines, gets more mileage out of its corporate title than its trackage. The museum possesses an incredibly ugly Baldwin 0-4-0T built in 1936. Originally a quarry engine, she is all the more fascinating since she appears larger and more ponderous than many 0-6-0T's. Since ugliness is a most desirable trait among saddle-tankers, this engine is a joy to watch — and photograph — in action. Like the Ohio museum, the Indianans use a trolley car to transport passengers — in this case, a 1917 interurban from the Chicago, Aurora and Elgin. A pleasant friendship has begun blossoming between railfan groups and old automobile enthusiasts, and many a Sunday will find the 1910 Maxwells and Stanley Steamers forming a convoy to the nearest operating steam locomotive, where the happy auto and rail buffs exchange rides on each other's motive power. These festivities are often accompanied by period costumes and picnic lunches. The Indiana Museum has known several such gatherings in its brief existence, and will undoubtedly have more in its promising future. *Below:* The Miami Railway Historical Society's Pacific performs every Sunday afternoon on the South Campus of the University of Miami. Until his death in November 1962, Mr. J. H. Johnson, a retired Florida East Coast engineer, was the patriarch of this operation. He knew No. 153 when she was new in 1922, and he wheeled her from Key West to Miami just two hours ahead of the 1926 hurricane which extensively damaged the line. He was one of the very few old enginemen who left his favorite locomotive secure in the knowledge that she would be safe from the torch. No. 153 is his best memorial.

RETIRED ENGINES WELL CARED FOR

The National Railroad Museum at Green Bay, Wisconsin, may soon become as popular an attraction as that town's fabulous football team. Its standard gauge steam engines include some of impressive dimensions, such as a U.P. Big Boy, a Santa Fe 2-10-4, a Milwaukee Road Northern and one of C&O's ubiquitous Kanawhas, as well as six smaller locomotives. On the facing page, the huge Santa Fe Texas-type and the Milwaukee 4-8-4 stand in silent allegiance to the flag which they and their forgotten sisters served so well during the Second World War and Korea. At *right:* James Srenaski, a teen-ager of the diesel generation, fires up the Museum's Lake Superior & Ishpeming Consolidation. He and his friend, Gregg Hodges, are assurance that the Museum's live steamers will be in good hands for many years to come. *Below:* The L. S. & I. 2-8-0 simmers between switching operations. The usual motive power is an 0-4-0T which pulls several wood coaches which are in an admirable state of preservation, complete with the original plush seats, oil lamps and wood paneling, from whence the railroad term "varnish" — passenger cars — originated. The equipment is displayed in a park-like setting spotted with trees and is a pleasant place to spend an afternoon. A trestle was recently built across Dutchman's Creek, and track is being extended. As soon as funds permit, a turntable and roundhouse will be built to house the growing roster.

REMINISCENCE OF NEW YORK CENTRAL STEAM

New York Central, originator of the 4-6-4 wheel arrangement which it named the Hudson, owned 275 of these great locomotives — more, perhaps, than all other North American railroads combined. The Hudson was widely acclaimed as the most beautiful locomotive ever built. Many people had other favorites, but fans of the Hudson felt the point could not be argued. While there are a number of 4-6-4's preserved, courtesy of the Burlington, the Santa Fe and the Nickel Plate, the New York Central, ignoring the pleas of railfans, scrapped every one of the original Hudsons. The road also cut up all twenty-seven of its post-war Niagaras, which were among the most modern and

handsome of 4-8-4's. The Central did, however, save an early 4-8-2 Mohawk which it recently sent to the Museum of Transport. But to railfans a Mohawk seemed a poor substitute indeed for a Hudson or a Niagara. Today, if one wishes to view a Hudson or a Niagara, he must rely on some of the splendid scale models available at model train stores. Here, at the Model Railroad Equipment Corporation in New York City, Erwin Frish holds one of Lionel's pre-war Hudson models. Like the prototype, the Lionel scale model was one of the most popular ever made. In the foreground is a brass Niagara, hand soldered in Japan and imported by Max Gray of California. It sells for about $200. Both locomotives are "0" gauge scale.

STATIONARY BOILERS

There are a number of locomotive boilers in service as stationary heating plants, such as the C.B.&Q. Mikado at the *rear left* of the photo *above*. In the foreground is a brand-new replacement boiler which never will be set on driving wheels as its builders intended. Its weight is slowly collapsing the weary flat car upon which it rests, and it will probably be scrapped by the steel company which owns it. *Right:* Two boilers from narrow-gauge Rio Grande 2-8-0's supply heat for the Company's shops at Chama, New Mexico. The six stripped Mikados *below* now see winter service generating steam to melt frozen ore at the Great Northern's yard at Allouez, Wisconsin. The steam is piped to the ore cars, some of which are visible in the yard, so they may be unloaded into Great Lakes freighters for transshipment to steel mills.

DEATH OF THE 6316

Before the diesel spread with great rapidity through every Class One railroad locomotive roster in America, the scrapping of steam engines was a routine matter. After thirty, forty, or even seventy years of service, an engine was sold for scrap as a newer one replaced it in service. The railroads would cut their locomotives up themselves or sell them to scrap dealers. It was only when the diesel began to send the steam locomotive to the acetylene torch in great numbers without replacement that people not usually associated with the scrapping process took note of its macabre fascination.

Only two per cent of the 44,000 steam engines in service on U.S. railroads at the end of World War II survived to the mid-sixties. Now the despondent steam fans have only a few hundred engines in parks and museums and the ever dwindling remnant of live steamers to console them. But what of the other 98 per cent? Here is the universal story of the real demise of steam.

Most railroads, after having sold a batch of engines to a scrap merchant, assembled them into a "death train," which was towed to the scrap yard. There, the locomotives were

stripped of any remaining valuable parts, such as bells, whistles and lights. They were left to rust on a rip track for days, months, or even years, until their turn at the torch.

The methods used in cutting up engines vary among different scrappers. Some may dismantle an engine part by part. Another common method is to cut a few components where the boiler joins the frame, then lift the entire boiler off the running gear and set it down where acetylene-torch-wielding "burners," as the scrap laborers are called, can cut it into convenient pieces three to five feet square. The most common method however, is that used by Northwestern Steel and Wire Company of Sterling, Illinois. On June 11th and 12th 1962, a Chicago, Burlington & Quincy 2-10-4 met this fate on Northwestern's scrap track. Here recorded are the pathetic last hours of engine No. 6316.

M-4 LINE-UP

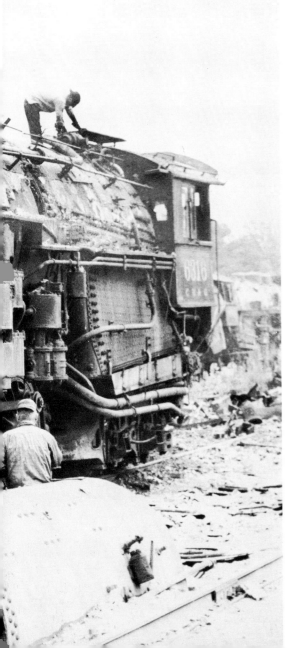

Above: Standing in a quarter-mile string of Burlington M-4 2-10-4's awaiting the torch, No. 6316 was next in line for scrapping. Coupled pilot to pilot with CB&Q 4-8-4 No. 5619, the big engine was cut up by two men in just fourteen working hours. *Left:* The men are cutting the boiler jacket so the asbestos lagging can be removed, then a lengthwise incision is made on the boiler itself. The ground is whitened by the boiler lagging of many engines previously scrapped here.

THE 6316 IS STRIPPED

Before she arrived on the scrap track, 6316's characteristic bell and oscillating lamp were salvaged from her smokebox front. Also missing were her marker lights, whistle and main rods Once the cut was made around the whole length of the boiler, the smokebox door was cut through. Next went her valve gear and connecting rods. After removing the cab, a gigantic traveling crane tore the center off the boiler with a long, repulsive creaking sound, amid a cascading cloud of boiler asbestos lagging. Burlington owned 28 of the M-4's, which were known as the Colorado type. 6316 and her sisters spent most of their lives pulling long coal freights on the CB&Q's Southern Illinois line. The M-4's were big engines; their total weight with loaded tender was close to 900,000 pounds, and they were the strongest of the CB&Q's freight engines. West Burlington Shops rebuilt and upgraded the 6300 series engines between 1935 and 1940. All this means nothing now, of course. 6316 is just 252 tons of scrap metal, worth about $5,000 — a minute fraction of her original cost.

THE BOILER GOES

Two more quick lifts and the crane has removed the whole top half of the boiler. Each section had two small holes cut in one side. Hooks from the crane were inserted, and the section yanked off, carried to a large open pit which the crane straddles, and lowered, to be cut up into smaller pieces. After removing the bottom of the firebox, the crane lifted out the boiler tubing. While the burners severed the trailing truck from 6316's frame, the crane removed the rest of the boiler. Once the men had made the vital cuts on the engine, it took the crane only two hours to drop the butchered remains of the M-4 among the fragments of dozens of steam locomotives lying in the pit. During scrapping no attention is paid to riveted or welded joints. The engine is cut into sections convenient for transport to the pit, where it is reduced to pieces suitable for Northwestern Steel's huge electric process melting buckets. Within hours, a magnetic crane loaded pieces of No. 6316 into gondolas bound for the mill. The remains of the M-4 were mixed with those of other engines and melted.

NEARLY FINISHED

Above: Just the bottom of the smokebox, the cylinder saddle, pilot, three pairs of driving wheels, and the pony truck remain of engine 6316. In the background are more locomotives and cars loaded with scrap wire — all awaiting the torch. The boiler section in the foreground protects acetylene valves (and lunchboxes) from falling debris.

LAST REMAINS

Below: Hardly more than four sets of wheels remain of the M-4. Then the burners immediately went to work on the 4-8-4, severing her piston rods. The great crane moved about in eerie silence on its four electric powered trucks. Resembling a massive mobile gallows, the crane crept about the pit, seeking additional victims for the furnaces.

MACABRE FASCINATION

Although nauseating to railfans, scrapping operations are fascinating to watch. Perhaps the same desires which motivate interest in adversity and misfortune compel even the most devout steam buffs to seek entrance to scrap yards. Some people, however, break down at the sight of these locomotives of once grand calling being destroyed, and workers report seeing railfans actually crying among the rows of condemned engines. The burners shed few tears however, although many agree that cutting up steam engines is not the most pleas-

ant of occupations. The following pages show the demise of engine 6316 in detail. *Above:* The piston rod at the moment of severing. The heavy crosshead is about to crash to the ground. Cutting the rod took few moments indeed, compared to the thousands of manhours of knowledge and skill involved in designing, building and aligning these massive parts when Baldwin constructed the engine in 1927. Note remnants of the valve gear and pipes hanging grotesquely from the frame, while loose pipes and brackets dangle above.

COLD COMPANIONSHIP

Above: The Burlington engines found little comfort in each other's company just before the end. In an environment of destruction and mountains of scrap steel, the men went to work on both engines at once. Efforts were concentrated on 6316 and a few hours later the Northern stood alone.

DISMANTLING THE FRONT END

Below: While one burner removed the headlight, the second severed all connections between the boiler and the engine pilot. *Right:* The first pieces of 6316 to arrive at the pit were her cab and boiler top. The remnants of many other locomotives are awaiting delivery to the melting pots.

A visit to an engine graveyard is a sobering experience. In the latter days of steam such a visit created a feeling of disaster and complete frustration to even casual steam fans. Here the most modern, the finest efforts of Baldwin, of Lima, of ALCO, waited for the last trip to the torch. There were Berkshires, Northerns, heavy Mikados and in other yards — Challengers, Alleghenies and even the supreme accomplishment — Union Pacific's Big Boy. Some engines were terribly mutilated long before their appointment with the burners. If a four-wheel trailing truck under the firebox of a 4-6-4 jumped the rails on the rip track, it was simply

cut off on the spot. An engine whose pilot overhung a switch lost everything in front of her cylinder castings.

When one ponders the thousands of man hours spent by the finest designers; the skill of the motive-power engineers; the labor of hundreds of workers in the erecting shops and repair areas, the finely developed and highly complex technology of a century of technical achievement, one feels a deep pain at the sickening groan as 20 tons of boiler top are ripped from the back of a proud engine. Castings of steel, massive but made to allow for tolerances of only a few thousandths of an inch, are cut apart and butchered.

To the condemned engines at Northwestern, the varnish and the hot-shot freight are dim in the memory of long ago. The fierce glow of a roaring fire and the throb of steam under pressure seem distant indeed. Now they are cold; killed in the prime of life; the scrap heap their reward for a magnificent job well done. Their intricate mechanisms rusted and smashed, these engines will soon be melted into new steel. The proud locomotives of story, of song, of great respect among all who knew them in action, will be lost in endless bales of wire at the far end of the steel mill.

DISMANTLING THE DRIVERS

Above: At the edge of the pit, a burner goes to work on the 6316's 64-inch driving wheels. Even when all the spokes have been cut, the whole axle may be hoisted ten feet up by the crane and dropped onto another set of drivers, fragmenting both. Shortly, one of Northwestern Steel's big 0-8-0 switch engines will spot the gondola cars on the adjoining track. The pieces will be loaded and 6316 will be brought to her funeral pyre. Twin sister 6315 was scrapped here just a few days before.

MASS GRAVE OF STEAM

Below: Less than three days after 6316 first felt the torch, her only discernible remnants were one set of driving wheels and her cab roof. The pit is reminiscent of a wartime mass grave; even the brilliance of the mid-afternoon sun radiates a macabre aspect to the scene. To heighten the eerie carnage, a man may appear from behind a cylinder saddle or a boiler wall; create a momentary flash of acetylene and white-hot metal, then disappear, leaving only a wisp of acrid smoke to mark his going.

UNFORTUNATE SISTER

Above: Their task with 6316 completed, the burners go to work on No. 5619. This engine was a sister of Burlington's renowned 5632 — the only passenger steam locomotive still owned by a Class One carrier to operate in the whole Mississippi Valley. The 5619 is far indeed from the fame which coincidence bestowed upon her fortunate sister; and she silently faced destruction with only the author to mourn her fate. The remaining pieces of the M-4 in the foreground were soon carried off by the sinister crane. *Right:* The electomagnet is attached to the hook, preparatory to lifting scrap into a waiting gondola car. The small wheels in the foreground are from 6316's trailing truck. They were demolished along with the driving wheels lying behind them. The cylinder unit to the right of the crane cables was also from the 2-10-4.

Northwestern operates eight ex-Grand Trunk Westerns 0-8-0 switchers which were pulled out of the scrap line. Burlington oscillating lamps were installed on the brows of these shifters. In the *background above,* dilapidated gondolas loaded with scrap wait to be fed into the large steel buckets in the mill. High gondola at *left* contains last remains of the 6316. A few hours later she will emerge as 252 tons of wire — or steel beams.

Progress? — perhaps, but at a high price. *Below:* The Grand Trunk Western's U-3b 4-8-4's were superb engines and a number of them were on Northwestern Steel's rip tracks. No. 6332 had suffered worse mutilation than most. The greater part of her boiler jacket was gone, her two-axle trailing truck had been amputated and rain had washed her lagging into a ghastly mantle of white, which covered her firebox. It was rumored that the

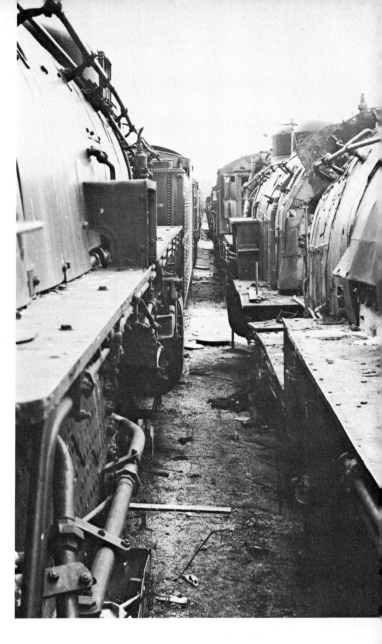

locomotive which pulled the last steam-powered scheduled passenger train in the United States, in 1960, was among the G T W engines in this line-up; but her identity was lost. Other G T W engines awaiting scrap included 4-8-2's, 4-6-2's, 2-8-2's, 2-8-0's, and 0-8-0's. *Right:* View from cab of C B & Q No. 5609 reveals endless array of Burlington 4-8-4's, 4-6-4's, 2-10-4's, and 2-8-2's; many without cabs, all without hope.

SCRAP YARD SCENES

The story of Northwestern Steel and Wire Company's scrap yard is among the saddest in railroading, but there are a few gratifying side-lights. The very nature of the work allows the company a choice selection of steam switch engines with which to replenish its fleet of eight 0-8-0's. Occasionally an old engineer will appear at the front office requesting admission to the yard. After wandering among the acres of rust and decay which were so recently great shining engines of thousands of horsepower, the engineer may find the faded number of the locomotive he once pampered and highballed across the divisions. Then, for

long moments he may sit once more in the cab, his hand on the throttle of memory. Such occurances are few, however, as defeat and despair are omnipresent.

After viewing the rows of mangled and torn engines, one can only hope that the scrapping process will proceed rapidly; for these magnificent locomotives actually seem to connote suffering and pain. The scrap yard was an unpleasant place to linger, even as the next locomotive was readied for the torch. She was still proud, and rust imparted a mystic quality to her last brief days; for she was, among iron horses, a thoroughbred — one of the last Nickel Plate Berkshires.

THE LAST ROUNDHOUSE

With the virtual disappearance of the steam locomotive from the railroads of the United States and Canada, fans have had to turn elsewhere to seek out the engines they love. For a while at least, one can still make a relatively inexpensive journey to Mexico City and the territory to the east and south, and there find whole divisions of the National Railways of Mexico blissfully innocent of diesel power.

The wonders yet to be encountered at the Valle de Mexico roundhouse are sufficient to prompt any steam-starved railfan to purchase a roomette on the Aztec Eagle (about one-third the usual U.S. rail fare) and make the 24-hour trip from Laredo to Mexico City, where the yards are but a 45-minute bus or taxi ride from the modern Buenavista Station. Immediately behind the glass and concrete administration building the hump, crowned by an ample tower, rises then drops into a modern classification yard. While a diesel switcher putters about, assembling cars for Northbound freights, trim 4-8-4 Niagaras simmer on the ready tracks, impatiently awaiting clearance.

Beyond the network of retarders, a 4-8-2, several 4-8-4's and possibly a 2-6-6-2, are getting up steam. Nearby another 4-8-4 may be taking on oil. These engines are unconcerned with the adjoining rip tracks now crammed with Consolidations recently retired and consigned to the inevitable fate.

The Ferrocarriles Nacionales de Mexico (N de M), as the government calls its railroad, maintains as modern a roundhouse as may be found in North America. This 34 stall arena of steam's final battle is a "must" for any railfan visiting Mexico.

OUT OF THE ROUNDHOUSE
After leaving the six-year-old Valle de Mexico roundhouse and taking on oil and water, a 4-8-4 trundles off to her waiting train.

POPPING OFF

Even in the most modern of facilities, steam locomotives still plot methods of asserting their individualistic personalities — usually to the despair
of the men to whom they are entrusted. A valve
jammed on a 4-8-0, resulting in the confusion pictured *above*. After half an hour the twelve-wheeler
calmed down long enough to enable a daring shop
worker to grope through the dense vapor to adjust
the valve amid shouts of "bravo" from his fellows.
At the *right,* a young Mexican roundhouse worker,
surrounded by the steel and steam which are the
environment of his calling, adjusts an airpump on
engine No. 3054. *Below,* one of the last operating
articulated steam locomotives in North America
clambers on to the turntable at dusk. These
2-6-6-2's are relatively small, once again illus-
trating that the strong and sophisticated are not
necessarily the survivors of adversity. Much larger
Big Boys and newer Y-6b's were scrapped north
of the border long before this picture was taken.

ROUNDHOUSE FUN

As the steam era draws toward the imminent finale in Mexico, so will these scenes of roundhouse daily routine; and the humorous deviltry among men which the steam locomotive always seemed to propagate. Once, as the author meditated upon a particularly intriguing 4-8-2, he was hit by a jet of valve oil ejected from the engine, twenty feet away. A Mexican hostler and the author were nearly doubled with laughter as the former closed the valve which had spit as if with deliberate aim. Mexican engineers will engage in a roundhouse bell and whistle duel at almost any provocation. The resulting din is overwhelming, with perhaps a half dozen whistles screaming in cacophony.

90

ROUNDHOUSE MEN AT WORK

The Mexican railroad workers are congenial "hams" who can sense a railfan's camera from afar. Trying to get them to work instead of posing is difficult if one's Spanish is limited to such phrases as "locomotura de vapor" (steam engine) and one or two other sayings. The welding crew *above* seemed unconcerned by the author's presence however, and the 4-8-4 at *left* was too absorbed in matters of a worker cleaning a pair of a sister's 70-inch drivers to pay attention to the doings of one Yanqui. The men in the 4-8-0 *below* paused in their labors to watch the author at his.

The Valle de Mexico roundhouse is much like hundreds of similar structures which once occupied terminal points in every part of the United States and Canada. Without exception, the roundhouses north of the Rio Grande have seen the last of big steam movements. All too soon they will disappear, since they are unsuited for economical diesel maintenance. Meanwhile they stand as silent monuments to the grand machines which once warmed their rafters, and the men who scurried about in an atmosphere of grease and oil; of steel, fire, and steam. Many have already been dismantled. Some now house bad-order rolling stock. Others are filled with the conquering diesels.

For the brief season left to steam power on this continent, the southern region of the National Railways of Mexico will be the source

4-8-4 BEING TURNED
A Niagara rides the turntable while a 4-8-2 simmers in the roundhouse. N de M purchased used engines from a number of U.S. lines, including a batch of FEC 4-8-2's and NKP 2-8-2's.

of its swansong and the place of its final going. Already these divisions of the N de M have assumed the characteristics of U.S. railroads during their motive power transition periods of the 1950s. Steam has been relegated to a secondary, and often to standby status in many areas. The 4-8-4's are still seen wheeling hot-shot freights and military trains, but diesels do virtually all passenger and yard work. With most of the older steam engines having been

READY TO ROLL

Four trains await clearance in the Valle de Mexico yard. Reminiscent of New York Central calendars of the 1920s, these 4-8-4's create a panorama never again to be seen north of the Rio Grande.

---

scrapped, the more modern power is beginning to go. Already 4-8-4's are being dismantled at the Aguascalientes Shops.

Steam is nearer extinction in Mexico than is readily evident. According to one N de M official, there were only 140 steam locomotives on the active roster in late 1962; less than those surviving in the United States. Unlike the U.S. engines which may be found in pairs and trios scattered about the nation, Mexico's steam engines are concentrated on the lines radiating out of Mexico City. Approximately twenty narrow gauge locomotives (mostly Baldwin 2-8-0's) handle the heavy traffic to Vera Cruz and probably will continue to do so for some time. The standard gauge engines are definitely doomed however, and the first six stalls of the Valle de Mexico roundhouse have already been converted for diesel maintenance.

To those who would see steam do final battle with the diesel; who would take one last walk through a roundhouse and absorb the exotic odors and exciting sounds which have faded with old memories, the time is short. The journey is indeed rewarding, the railroad quite accommodating (if prior arrangements are made) and the steam engine is beautiful to behold in her dying glory.

STEAM SAFARI

Almost a decade ago, when the diesel had already swallowed up approximately 85 per cent of the work of railroading, and the victory was not complete, Editor David P. Morgan of *Trains Magazine* voiced the concern of all the faithful in these words in his April 1954 issue:

"The steam locomotive in 1954 is reminiscent of some prehistoric monster unable to cope with the tide of evolution – a hapless, harried, hunted creature, dying off in large numbers, facing total extinction. The simple curb of knocking down coaling stages and water tanks, filling in ash pits, and cooling backshop forges has fenced steam off hundreds, even thousands, of miles of main line — forever. The very foundries which hatched it less than a decade ago now spawn its killer. Practically everywhere anything with a stack on one end and a firebox under the other is fair game for the torch, and depletion of the reserve only boosts the bounty.

"And as in any upheaval so sudden and so widespread, established values are upset and the strongest no longer have prior claim to survival. Wabash 2-6-0's puffed along a Missouri branch months after the road's Mountains and Northerns had been put out to pasture. Pacifics were wheeling commuters homeward on Rock Island and Erie when these systems had been swept clean of steam freight and yard power long since. So it was with hulking simple articulateds, shark-nosed duplex-drives, and horsepower-heavy Berkshires; youth availed them not. The intricate valve motion or the high-pressure boiler that excited so much rapt attention when new was likely the first to give way before the limited maintenance law that forecast the end.

"But no matter how stormed, the shrines of steam toppled. Chicago, Kansas City, St. Louis, Atlanta, Los Angeles...Sayre, Billerica, Huntington . . . Ozarks, Rockies, Blue Ridges . . . Cajon, Crawford Notch, Saluda — the rule has become the exception. For those who found in steam more than mere machinery, who rejoiced in its glory age — for those, the frustration of its absence has been impossible to either deny or resolve. The dilemma has brought forth, among the faithful, a sort of steam safari, a game of cat-and-mouse played with the diesel to see who can get there first."

Later, much later, when steam was accounting for less than 0.01 per cent of railroad work, Morgan wrote this to the author: "The frustration has increased immeasurably since those days. *If* one had the funds and the time then, he could still witness the passage of a Central Hudson or a UP 4-12-2, and of course steam in some abundance was to be had north in Canada and south in Mexico. But today the active steam locomotive is an exhibitionist, no longer accountable for the orthodox work of railroading, but paid simply to perform. There are moments when the circus at-

THE STAR PERFORMER

One of the steam locomotives which is now merely "an exhibitionist" is Nevada Northern ten-wheeler No. 40 (*above*). The last operating steam locomotive in Nevada, she was taken out of retirement on August 28, 1962, to star in the picture "Windows of Heaven" being filmed on location by Brigham Young University.

mosphere is a bit thick, for the 4-8-4 recalled by the fans may wear too much makeup or lay down smoke at photo stops which would once have endangered her fireman's job, or even talk it up too sharply because the hogger hasn't notched her up, out of regard to the sound recorders. And yet the excitement today is more intense than ever. In the back of everyone's mind are the questions almost too awful to contemplate: Suppose they don't renew her flues next year, what *then?* Is this *really* the Missabe's last steam excursion? Has U.P. really earmarked *this one* for park preservation at year's end?

"It is because we cannot count on tomorrow that the faithful are so thankful for today. If this be a dilemma, then we are making the most of it."

ALONG THE "'POSSUM TROT LINE"

Although still very much in revenue freight service, the Reader Railroad's 2-6-2, No. 11 (*right*), also wheels tourists through the bayous of Arkansas.

SHORT LINE FREIGHT

The short line railroad has been an important feature of the American landscape ever since the inception of railroading. Usually built for limited use; such as connecting a mine or industry with a Class I railroad, or providing isolated communities with outside contact, each short line is individualistic in its quaint mannerisms.

Basically rural in locale and casual in operating procedure, short lines are the most romantic and fascinating of all roads for the fans, and publications dealing with their off-beat habits are the most popular reading matter for the *aficionado*. A short line is usually less than fifty miles long (often only two to ten miles) and boasts but two or three locomotives, a caboose and until quite recently, a combination baggage and passenger car. These curious little roads seldom own but one or two decrepit cars which normally see service in maintenance-of-way work, which, in the case of most short lines, is rare indeed.

A short line normally operates one round-trip five days weekly; but sometimes as little as one or two journeys a week are made. Right up until dieselization, the standard motive power for these railroads was the popular Baldwin Consolidation of pre-1915 vintage, although ten-wheelers, 4-4-0's, Army surplus 0-6-0's, Prairies, Moguls and an occasional Mikado were also to be found trundling axle-deep in weeds or churning through the mud. Since profits are usually marginal, upkeep is limited to the barest expenses necessary to maintain minimum safety requirements on most short lines, and even less on many.

There are several hundred short lines still operating in the United States, but most of them have turned to 44-ton diesels or second-

LAST SUMMER OF BEVIER & SOUTHERN STEAM

On a stifling August day, with the temperature at 100 degrees, a Bevier & Southern 2-8-2 chuffs anxiously toward the water tank to quench her thirst. Afterwards, she will switch the hoppers left at the Burlington interchange, preparatory to another run to the coal mine which is the railroad's main source of revenue.

hand road units for their motive power requirements. A dwindling number of these little lines still rely on steam locomotives; either as primary power or stand-by for diesels. In recent years, even most of the steam powered short lines have lost much of their country atmosphere after grading their rights-of-way and laying heavier rail. Some, such as the Graham County Railroad and the Morehead & North Fork, still maintain the timeless vestiges which, except for an occasional cushioned-underframe boxcar which may stray onto the line, have left them much as they were thirty years ago.

Aside from the conversion to diesel power, the greatest change affecting the remaining short lines since World War II is the total disappearance of the mixed train, which consisted of both passenger and freight cars. Today, only two mixed trains are listed in the *Official Guide,* compared to several hundred which still saw service in the mid-'40's. Just one of these, the Moscow, Camden & San Augustine, in eastern Texas, is of the traditional variety, with steam on the head-end, and a wood combine at the rear. But even this pleasant circumstance is a curiosity, for the small Mikado is only recalled from retirement about twenty days a year; when the regular diesel is being serviced. The only all-steam mixed train to grace the pages of the *Guide* is that of the Reader Railroad, 250 miles from the M C & S A, in Arkansas. Steel passenger equipment of a later era is used on the Reader.

The mixed train seems on the verge of a Renaissance. In the Spring of 1963, Nelson Blount was negotiating for 18 miles of trackage (Bellows Falls to Grassetts, Vermont) from the bankrupt Rutland Railway. He planned to operate a steam-powered mixed train, common-carrier, over the line. Other short lines around the nation may join this trend eventually.

DIXIE SIMPLICITY IN ALABAMA

There is, in deepest Alabama, a 14-mile railroad known as the Mobile & Gulf, and located over 200 miles from either Mobile or the Gulf of Mexico. Perhaps the most beautiful little locomotive still in steam, Mogul No. 97 appears to be endeavoring to impress the photographer as she tows an ancient gondola near Brownville, Alabama.

STEAM IN THE VIRGINIAS

At Fort Eustis, Virginia, the U.S. Army Transportation Corps maintains several immaculate "G.I." locomotives of 0-6-0 and 2-8-0 wheel arrangements. These engines are quite active, for this is the last place in the United States where men are formally trained to completely service steam engines. The most popular locomotive is 2-8-0 No. 611, shown here as she strutted about the post in mid-Summer 1962. Her whistle is an exact replica of Casey Jones' famous "whippoorwill" whistle, and was made by Sergeant Burl F. Wylie of the 714th Railway Operating Battalion. Sergeant Wylie actually measured the original whistle at the Casey Jones Museum, then built this beautifully mellow-toned replica out of boiler tubing in only two days. *At right,* Consolidation No. 4 of West Virginia's Buffalo Creek & Gauley pulls one boxcar and fifty hoppers toward the coal mines at Widen on a warm Winter day in 1963.

LAST OF STEAM IN NEVADA

At right, the last steam locomotive to operate in Nevada, ten-wheeler No. 40 of the Nevada Northern, made one of her rare appearances under steam in August 1962. She has been fired up once or twice annually for movie crews and fan groups since her replacement by diesel power. She made one more trip, for the annual convention of the Nevada Bar Association on September 29, the day before her flues expired. The 4-6-0, built by Baldwin in 1910, was spared the torch, temporarily at least, while the railroad applied for a flue extension and contemplated the costs of a complete overhaul. The wooden baggage car and coach are usually stored indoors since the N.N. no longer offers rail passenger service. The railroad has also placed a 2-8-0 on display in East Ely, where the general office and shops of the N.N. are located.

IN THE TWILIGHT DAYS OF MICHIGAN STEAM

In 1962, the Lake Superior & Ishpeming still had two operational Consolidations on the property at Marquette, Michigan: Nos. 20 and 23. *At right,* where a well-manicured lawn grows right to the edge of the turntable pit, No. 23, called out of semi-retirement to replace a disabled diesel, rode the turntable during the last days of L.S.& I. steam. Five recently retired sisters awaited the oblivion of scrap a short distance behind the roundhouse. Unless plans to run steam specials on the Big Bay branch were realized, it would be a short time indeed, before the Lake Superior & Ishpeming would retire the last of steam on the upper Michigan peninsula. No. 24, a twin sister of 20 and 23, was operating at the National Railroad Museum in Green Bay, Wisconsin. Soon the engines of the Duluth & Northeastern would be the last revenue steam in the Great Lakes area; and their futures were very insecure. Their days were numbered.

100

NEAR-EXTINCT SPECIES IN MINNESOTA

The ore-hauling railroads of northern Michigan, Wisconsin, and Minnesota were among the last to surrender to diesel power. Long after the steam greats such as Pennsy and C&O had dropped out, the Missabe's huge 2-8-8-4's still wheeled iron ore to the docks at Duluth. By 1960, that too, was past, but steam was still in evidence in the beautiful wilderness between the Straits of Mackinac and the western end of Lake Superior. *At left,* No. 16 of the Duluth & Northeastern, a 1913 Baldwin 2-8-0 of classic short line style, switched around huge wood stacks at Cloquet, Minnesota. Nearby, No. 29, an ex-U.S. Army 0-6-0 of 1944 Lima stock, shunted Northern Pacific boxcars.

MID-AFTERNOON WATER STOP

Above, at a water stop near Elizabethton, Tennessee, an ex-Southern Railways 2-8-0, now the property of the East Tennessee & Western North Carolina, takes on water. The railroad, only nine miles in length since the abandonment of its famous "Tweetsie" narrow-gauge portion, owns two well kept Consolidations, Nos. 207 and 208. The ET&WNC connects with the Southern and the Clinchfield at Johnson City, Tennessee.

STEAM BOWS OUT OF MISSOURI

Until 1962, the motive power of the Bevier & Southern consisted of a pair of 2-8-2's leased from the Burlington. The road also owned two Moguls in standby service. One CB&Q engine, No. 4943, was returned after estimates indicated that major repairs would be a prohibitive expense. *Below,* 2-6-0 No. 112 waited outside the roundhouse for the diesels which finally displaced these last steam engines operating in Missouri.

THE EXCITEMENT OF STEAM

One of the great thrills in steam days was to stand upon a railroad underpass as a locomotive, working hard on tonnage or wheeling a fast passenger train, blasted underneath. The whole structure would shake, and smoke and steam would billow all around, momentarily cutting off all vision except swirling grey and white vapors. Suddenly it would begin to subside, and the front of the roaring, clanking engine would appear through the confusion. Then, amid the rhythmic clickety-clack of car wheels on rail joints, the smoke would dissipate, the bridge structure would cease shaking, and the locomotive, her train now visible, would flash out of sight beyond the curve. Few experiences, short of riding in the cab, could compare with it. Here, enacted one more time by Kentucky & Tennessee Railway Mikado No. 10, is this timeless show, as the 2-8-2 fights a cut of hoppers upgrade toward the Southern Railway at Stearns, Kentucky, on a wet January afternoon.

STEAM IN THE SOUTH AND SOUTHWEST

At the upper left, Mikado No. 7 of the Magma Arizona puffs away from the Magma Copper Co. plant after leaving a cut of cars. The railroad, owned by the copper interests, also operates a 2-8-0 which appears huge by comparison with the small 2-8-2. A Baldwin 2-6-0, recently retired, was placed on permanent display at the plant in Superior, Arizona. The smokeboxes of the locomotives are coated with a copper-based paint which gives them a handsome — and a very original — appearance. The Moscow, Camden & San Augustine, which runs a mere seven miles between Moscow and Camden, Texas, and never did reach the San Augustine of it corporate title, is nevertheless of vital importance to students of railroading. *The lower photo opposite* shows the MC&SA's venerable wood combine, built by the Long Island Rail Road in 1898, trailing a string of boxcars and the MC&SA 2-8-2, No. 14. Due

to water in the fuel oil, the engine had stalled on the grade, and was pausing to build up steam at this time. *Above,* the 2-8-2, called out of retirement at year's end to fill in for the diesel, pulls a cut of cars out of the yard at Camden. The cabbage-stacked logging engines, perhaps the last survivors of this type, are among nine locomotives of six different wheel arrangements rusting in the yard. *Below,* Virginia Blue Ridge 0-6-0 No. 9 leaves Piney River, Virginia, with a train to meet the Southern Railway at Tye River, seven miles eastward. The VBR has two other ex-U.S. Army 0-6-0's in running condition, as well as a similar engine and a 1907 Baldwin 2-8-0 on the rip track. In 1962 the Virginia Blue Ridge had ample parts on hand to keep its steam engines operational throughout the decade. (No. 9 also appears on three pages in the first chapter). VBR will probably be the last short line in the East to dieselize.

MISSISSIPPIAN RAILWAY

Although the Buffalo Creek & Gauley, the Kentucky and Tennessee and the Virginia Blue Ridge all own more serviceable locomotives (three each), the Mississippian Railway is the longest (24 miles) all-steam road in the entire South. Its two Consolidations of obvious Frisco ancestry are kept in topnotch condition by a unique team of two brothers. In a pleasant return to a nearly-forgotten 19th Century railroad custom, each man has his "own" engine. Jim Carlisle normally operates No. 76, while his brother Frank is in charge of No. 77. Depending on whose locomotive is in service on any given day, one man is engineer and the other serves as conductor. The Carlisle's father was even more versatile; having been superintendent, master mechanic and engineer — all at once. The Mississippian, which runs from Amory to Fulton, in the northeast corner of the state, is known as "the Bentonite Road," in reference to its primary freight, a clay bonding material used in foundry work. *At left,* a fireman's eye view of No. 77 hard at work. *Above,* No. 77, a Baldwin graduate of 1920, leaves the enginehouse at Amory for the first time after three months of undergoing an overhaul. Sister 76, in the adjoining stall, will be repaired next. If the Bentonite Road were forced to dieselize, steam would be vanquished in Mississippi. Fortunately, however, the Mississippian is quite content with its trim 2-8-0's and has been stocking whatever spare parts it can locate. Big brother Frisco, whose number plates still adorn the smokeboxes of Nos. 76 and 77, has placed No. 1529, a 4-8-2, on display in Amory.

107

MORE STEAM IN DIXIE

At left, during her waning months of steady employment, an ex-Southern Railway 0-6-0 of Kentucky's Morehead & North Fork crossed a bridge with hoppers in tow. A diesel was to take over in 1963, dispossessing the 1905 ALCO switcher. *Below,* the Rockton & Rion acquired fame in rail circles for purchasing steam locomotives as late as 1961. The granite-hauling road runs 12 miles from Rockton, South Carolina, to Anderson Quarry, and operates the three locomotives pictured here (a 2-8-2, an 0-4-0T and a 2-8-0), as well as a 1906 Baldwin 2-8-2, which at the time was receiving heavy repairs after having its smokebox smashed in by a runaway hopper car loaded with 65 tons of stone. *On the opposite page,* in a late summer idyl of Arkansas backwoods, a light Prairie type locomotive displays all the beauty and peacefulness that once was short line railroading. The practice of filling the tank from a pond when necessary, the serenity of a mid-afternoon pause in the forest, all lend an air of the almost vanquished era of steam in the deep South, which, thanks to a calculated business risk taken by T.W.M. Long, president of the Reader Railroad, may be available to the public for years to come. In December 1962, the Reader inaugurated a mixed train service three days weekly. The journey, to a picnic grove being built at Waterloo, 23 miles (and 126 bridges) from Reader, is one of the finest rail trips in the U.S. This is a genuine common-carrier mixed train, run year round, and the last one entirely steam powered to operate north of the Rio Grande. A trip on the Reader is a magnificent experience, and passengers can take advantage of a fine picnic grove at Waterloo, while the 2-6-2's switch at the asphalt plant.

CAROLINA SHORT LINE

Among the surviving short lines still in steam, few are more fascinating than the Graham County Railroad in western North Carolina. It is the daily run of a road such as this — routine, yet extraordinary — which thrills the short line enthusiast. The informality, the simplicity of operations, the legendary ingenuity of small-time railroading, are all apparent as the little Shay makes her daily-except-Sunday trip

A SHAY AT WORK AND AT REST

Above: Shay No. 1926, her spark arrester netting behind the stack, waits patiently in a January morning drizzle, while sister 1925 is receiving a major overhaul in the adjoining shop building. At *left,* high above U.S. Route 19, the three-truck Shay assembles her train from cars left by the Southern at Topton. Few Eastern roads still in steam can match the splendor of scenery on the G.C.R.R.

between Robbinsville and Topton, where she meets the Southern's Murphy branch.

Formerly part of a logging railroad complex, twelve miles of the Bemis Lumber Company's line remains as a common carrier, and still serves as such even though trucks now haul timber to the mill. G.C.'s rolling stock consists of several bad-order flatcars and a decaying second-hand caboose, obviously of Southern Railway ancestry. The slow but powerful Shays are necessary in these mountains, for a standard engine could hardly pull itself up the grades, not to mention the eight loaded cars the Shays often handle.

The Graham County Railroad emerged in 1925 after a succession of lumbering ventures around southwest Carolina resulted in the Bemis Lumber Company moving to Robbinsville. The railroad began hauling finished lumber to the Southern junction at Topton behind

STEEP CLIMB

Left: Clinging precariously to the frail sixty-pound rail, a train climbs the six per cent grade over the Snowbird Mountains towards Robbinsville, on the edge of the Great Smokies. *Above:* The front view shows the off-center boiler; designed to counter-balance the weight of the Shay's three cylinders, which are all mounted vertically on the right side.

a brand-new Shay delivered by Lima in 1925. The seventy ton "side-winder," as Shays are appropriately nicknamed, was numbered for the year of her acquisition. Sister No. 1926 was actually bought in 1940. To confuse the numbering system further, her front plate tabs her as 3229. This occurred after she was hit head-on by a runaway car. She was repaired using a number plate from a narrow gauge Shay scrapped at Robbinsville.

The G.C. is one of the most fascinating runs yet in steam. When 1926 challenges the six per cent grade north of Topton, her rumbling exhaust echoes for miles up the valley. Smoke is often hurled two hundred yards up into the clear sky which broods a deep blue over that indiscernible line where the Smoky Mountains merge with the Snowbird range. Here all the ingredients that compose railroad legends join to reward the more adventuresome of railfans. There is the path through 200 yards of timber where a loaded boxcar went off a cliff a few years back. Since the tightly-packed lumber kept the car rigid, most damage was incurred by ladders, grab irons, and the catwalk. Bulldozers then dragged it back up to the track. It was repaired and sent to the Southern.

There are several modest bridges constructed of two I-beams on concrete abutments, but the Shays are just as apt to be seen towing huge modern 55-foot steel chipwood cars through a stream as over it. On rainy winter days, sections of the track may sink several inches into the mud, always reappearing after the weary caboose has passed. The few riders on the G.C.R.R. travel in the caboose or the engine cab.

One of the last survivors of many standard and narrow gauge shortlines which once meandered around these mountains, the Graham County will probably keep its Shays in steam for years to come. The company is proud of its sidewinders and the power that once enabled 1926 to win a timely victory over an embarrassed Southern diesel engineer by pushing his whole train up the Topton grade. Nobody disparages the hefty Shays anymore, but increasing difficulty in obtaining spare parts may someday bring the unwanted echo of a diesel horn to the Snowbird Mountains.

MOUNTAIN ENGINEER

Bible-quoting engineer Ed Collins (*right*) is a veteran of many years service on the Graham County Railroad. Here he looks over his train as it rounds a curve and crosses one of the informal bridges.

MINOR DERAILMENT

On January 6, 1962, three cars derailed during the return from Topton. The reason: a fifty-foot boxcar loaded with cement for a contractor in Robbinsville, proved too heavy for light rails spiked to decaying ties on a mud roadbed. Overloaded, the car weighed sixty tons. Fortunately, the maximum speed on this part of the line is only nine miles per hour, otherwise the car *below* would surely have followed the ties into the stream. *Above:* Crewmen with crescent shaped rerailers on their shoulders head for the derailed cars. Although lightweight, rerailers are rugged and can support great loads.

RERAILING

About fifty yards of one rail turned on its side as the cars bounced along the ties, cutting some of them in two. Here is the rerailing operation as the cement-laden car is slowly pulled back onto the rails. After uncoupling the car on the bridge, the crew wedged rerailers under the wheel flanges of the rear truck of the cement car. As the Shay pulled the car, it slowly eased onto the rails, only to collapse another thirty feet of broken rail. After several attempts at rerailing in this primitive — but usually effective — manner, the engine had dragged the car another twenty yards, bending rails and chewing up ties on the way. Various local mountain folk, while passing by, stopped to proffer advice of dubious value. Then a small but vocal group raised enough hullabaloo and muscle and the car was back on the tracks — for this trip at least.

ON TO ROBBINSVILLE!

Above: The brakeman signals engineer Ed Collins at the moment of rerailment. When asked the frequency of these mishaps, a crewman replied: "Oh we haven't had one for several days now." Al-though recurrent, these derailments are rarely serious. Leaving four cars and the caboose stranded on the other side of the broken rails, the balance of the train continued on to Robbinsville, two hours late. Mr. Collins commented that they would have to leave the other cars "till Monday, when we can get the yard crew down to rerail 'em."

SMOKE, STEAM AND SNOW

If the steam locomotive was interesting to observe during the mild seasons, she was fascinating under sub-freezing conditions. The chilled atmosphere accented every drop of vapor which spewed from valves, pumps and exhausts. When the thermometer descended toward zero, steam condensation swirled in elusive wisps around the boiler, depositing silver ice on wheels and rods. The steam engine was at her esthetic best on the cold clear winter days of the northern United States; and in Canada she would go wild to impress her admirers with huge plumes of the whitest exhaust imaginable.

Even the most humble of steam locomotives — the industrial tank engine — could turn in a performance comparable to a Mikado or a Pacific. Of course, by the winter of 1961, when most of these pictures were taken, large engines were seldom to be seen under steam in snow and ice. For some reason, fantrips are usually a summertime thing and the locomotives used on these excursions have acquired the habit of hibernating during winter (except in Canada and on the Burlington).

While the big 4-8-4's sleep in various roundhouses, the six 0-6-0T "Docksides" of the Brooklyn Eastern District Terminal work through each winter practically within the shadow of the Empire State Building. The B.E.D.T. is unique in several respects. Its eleven miles of track which serve waterfront industries in the heart of New York City (a mile from the East River boundary of Brooklyn, Queens and Manhattan) have no physical union with any other railroad; all connections are by carfloats — barges which are capable of carrying a dozen or more freight cars. Until several operating rail museums opened upstate, these little tankers were the only active steam locomotives left in New York State. Like most steamers, however, their service is about over.

TANK ENGINES AT DUSK

Side-tanker No. 12 escorts No. 15 from a carfloat
which one of the B.E.D.T's tugboats has just
brought in. It is a cold wet evening in February,
and the latter engine has returned from a day's
switching around the Brooklyn Navy Yard. The
pair of ghostly engines will trundle to the shop
tracks where they will be refueled and serviced.

DECEMBER BLIZZARD

Above: Saddle-tank engines 14 and 15 wait out a raging December blizzard as gusts of wind pile snow around them. The water formed by condensation on the hot boilers has created a fine array of icicles on the running boards and rods of both engines. Despite the absence of plows and pilot trucks, the little tankers made many a four-foot snowdrift fly before their persistent efforts during the four major snow storms of 1960-61.

SNOWY WAIT

Below: B.E.D.T. tug "Invincible" is tied up alongside the tracks. An engine with snow piled high against her frame patiently simmers while men work to clear frozen switches. All of these engines are oil-fired. Five were built by Porter, while No. 10, the oldest on the roster, is Baldwin's handiwork. An ancient wood boxcar with steel ends, truss rods and arch-bar trucks is also on the property; but now is used only for storage purposes.

AWAITING THE TORCH

Unused, and being cannibalized for spare parts, old Baldwin-built No. 11 stands in solitude as snow drifts high on her cold cylinders and empty boiler. A year and a half passed before she was finally cut to pieces; never having been moved.

CLEAR AND VERY COLD

Backing into an icy wind which is blowing off the East River, an 0-6-0T is about to begin towing cars from a barge. The temperature was fourteen degrees, and chilled spray cascading from the pilings coated the rails with ice. The engine crews were warm enough in the enclosed cabs, and the brakemen climbed aboard frequently to keep warm. On days such as this, work was tedious and hot coffee was in abundance. These little engines required no tenders since their small fuel supply could be amply transported in a bunker at the rear of the cab. The water tanks were either alongside the boiler or slung over it, like a saddle. The Brooklyn Eastern District Terminal set its first diesel to work on October 22, 1962. Two of the steam engines had been sold; the rest were to be cannibalized for parts until late 1964, when the B.E.D.T. was to become just another anonymous terminal road, whose charm had been destroyed by the clatter of a few colorless diesel switch engines.

121

LITTLE WORKHORSES

Within the United States there are about 2,000 industrial, tourist or other railroads not listed in the *Official Guide*. The vast majority of these small pikes have acquired the diminutive 44-ton diesels or some other such colorless motive power to replace steam switchers, tank engines or Shays. Yet such businesses as Willis Gravel, Calcasieu Paper and Deer Island Granite, still rely on steam power, as do the Klickitat and the Ely Thomas Lumber companies. None of these railroads is mentioned in the *Guide,* because they are not common-carriers and are not subject to I.C.C. regulations. These roads are often in a fascinating state of decay.

Some of the railroads here, such as the Brooklyn Eastern District Terminal and the Brimstone, are, in fact, listed in the *Guide* and therefore may be regarded as having legitimate short line status along with the lines chronicled in Chapter 8. However, since this book is more concerned with motive power than with the legal bureaucracy of the Interstate Commerce Commission, it makes more sense to group all roads which operate slow switching-type locomotives in one chapter reserved for those near-forgotten little workhorses, from whose noble efforts the elements of huge freight trains are formed. The trains which the big power ultimately pulled across the nation often had their beginnings courtesy of quaint little saddle-tanks or outboard-geared Shays.

Basically a switch engine was intended to operate at slow speeds (hence the absence of pilot wheels which were needed to guide the rigid driver wheel-base of longer, faster engines around curves). With all of its weight on the drivers a switcher, or "yard goat," also exerted great traction for its size. When an engine was expected to wander out of the yards

and climb rugged hills with sharp curves, chances are that one of the famous Shays was used. What they lacked in speed, they possessed in power. Little railroads often used second-hand power, especially in the last years of steam. Hence, a 4-6-0, which was formerly a fast road engine, may be found switching around a gravel pit, or an 0-6-0 may be chugging on a well graded mainline with a regular freight drag. When the engine was available, the buyers were more interested in condition and age than in builders intentions, or the by-gone glories of a locomotive's past assignments.

TENNESSEE SHAYS

The Appalachian Mountain area was the only major stronghold of steam remaining during the early 1960's. Within a four-hour drive from Bluefield, West Virginia, in the area where five states meet, approximately thirty steam locomotives operated as late as 1962 on about a dozen short line lumber and coal roads. The Appalachian range also includes the narrow gauge tourist roads, the Tweetsie, the Rebel, and the Cherokee Wonderland. This Valhalla of steam was one of the chief operating areas of the Shay geared engine — and still is. Pennsylvania with her East Broad Top, her Strasburg and her Reading Rambles is just to the north. On this page, two Shays of the Brimstone Railroad slowly cool down at an old wooden engine house after switching around New River, Tennessee. The Shays, Nos. 35 and 36, are of 1910 origin. They fulfilled the motive power needs of the Brimstone by moving hundreds of carloads of Tennessee coal monthly for transshipment to various points of the nation. Steam engines such as these are performing a dwindling role in the transportation economy of the Southeast.

TWO MORE ELUDE THE TORCH

Beyond the jurisdiction of the Interstate Commerce Commission, the Twin Seams Mining Company operated a Shay of great antiquity in appearance. This engine, No. 5, which came from the roster of the Meadow River Lumber Company, of Rainelle, West Virginia, in 1958, is now the main engine used for hauling coal out of the mines near Kellerman, Alabama. *At upper left,* after one of her many derailments, the three-truck Shay has her shaft replaced while a welder repairs a cracked brake beam. Then, traversing the undulating iron through deep Alabama forests which are protected from the Shay's wrath by a sizable spark arrester in the home-made diamond stack, No. 5 leads a cut of loaded hoppers toward the Gulf, Mobile & Ohio junction at Fox River, sixteen miles from Kellerman. *Above,* on a subfreezing December morning at Perry, Florida, 2-6-2 No. 1 (Baldwin, 1914) of the J. C. Turner Lumber Co., sat forlornly among the buildings and equipment of an abandoned mill. A few months later she was sold to an operating rail museum. This photo was taken through the cab of engine No. 2, which was scrapped previously.

SADDLE-TANKERS AND A SHAY

In and around major cities, it is often the practice to maintain terminal railroads. They are small switching roads, sometimes owned jointly by the Class One lines they connect, often independent, and until dieselization, usually operating nothing larger than an 0-8-0. After the retirement of Dallas Union Terminal's dapper six-coupled switcher, the Brooklyn Eastern District Terminal remained as the sole terminal road in the U.S. to be 100 per cent steam powered. But not for long; a diesel now plies the sidings between the factories which line Kent Avenue, and the days of the tank engines are waning. *At left,* the ubiquitous Manhattan skyline forms a backdrop for the East River setting where the 0-6-0T's are resting on a Sunday afternoon in early Spring. *At the lower left,* the Reading Locomotive Shop's 0-6-0T, whose renown is eclipsed by the company's famous 4-8-4's (their tenders are visible in the roundhouse), trundles past the coal dock in Reading, Pennsylvania. The saddle-tanker's job is to switch dead diesels around the shops. *Below,* plying the forty-pound rail of the Ely Thomas Lumber Company's yard in Fenwick, West Virginia, No. 2, a 65-ton Shay built in 1906, began her day's switching as she wearily rumbled between stacks of lumber, a stream of water from her leaking tank marking her passage. Another Shay is stored serviceable.

A STUDY IN ESTHETICS

One of the elements contributing to the appeal and subtle beauties of the steam locomotive was its varied surface texture. From the mirror-smooth piston rods and headlight reflector, to the rough steel castings of wheel centers and frame, the steam engine in close-up was never lacking variety. The sharp angular forms complemented by the basic cylindrical shapes of the lo-comotive tended to make it appear vibrant and powerful even when standing still. Even such a small locomotive as a B.E.D.T. dockside (*above*) could easily inspire a contemporary painter with its bold design elements. The flaking paint, mud and rust accent the effects of rugged steel and of dried oil on the switcher's running gear. The monotonous sheen of diesel hoods fade by comparison.

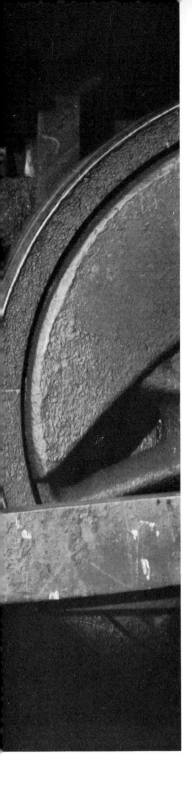

GHOSTLY IN A MAINE FOG

The time is past when virtually every stone quarry boasted at least one 0-4-0T to haul flat cars and gondolas loaded with tons of granite or marble to be processed. Now, if the railroads haven't been abandoned for trucks, small industrial diesel locomotives perform the tasks. In a few remote quarries, such as the Deer Island Granite Corporation, steam may still move the huge blocks of stone. *Below,* running on several hundred yards of track on the island off the coast of Maine, a 1931 Vulcan 0-4-0T emerges from a thick fog.

THE LAST TIMBER-HAULING STEAM ENGINE

The last steam locomotive to haul logs out of the North Woods will undoubtedly be a well-groomed ninety-ton Shay, No. 7 of the Klickitat Log and Lumber Company. The last of 3,000 steamers which only a few years ago hauled millions of feet of timber to the mills, No. 7 makes a 37-mile daily round trip between Klickitat, Washington, near the Columbia River, and the reload, where trucks bring fresh timber out of the woods. For the trip up, No. 7 usually hauls about 35 empty log cars to be loaded with timber transferred from the trucks. In the early afternoon, she brings the loaded cars down to the unload at the storage pond (*above*) where they are dumped, one by one. Livestock, particularly deer, are always on the right-of-way (*left*) and the rifle which is a standard fixture in the cab of the Shay during the hunting season, sees good service. In recent years, the company has embarked on the policy of allowing railfans to ride the tank of the Shay. There is an old automobile seat which accommodates four passengers, the ride is beautiful, the management and crew extremely friendly and for a while at least, here is the last chance to watch a genuine logging railroad in steam.

SWITCHERS AT A PAPER MILL

In 1962, there were still at least five steam locomotives operating on four different railroads in
Louisiana. When the national status of steam was
reviewed, that made Louisiana one of the foremost states in numbers of operable steam engines.
By year's end, however, the last active steamer of
Paulson Spence's Louisiana Eastern (page 48)
had gotten the torch, leaving the two wee Prairie
engines of the Calcasieu Paper Co. (*below*) and
the two ten-wheelers on the following pages. Calcasieu's little oil burners sported tenders of unusual configuration. They switched pulpwood cars
around the mill at Elizabeth. The two engines,
said to be converted woodburners, had been working at the mill for over a quarter century.

CAROLINA SADDLE-TANKER

The Edgmoor & Manetta, in South Carolina, is a
prime example of short line simplicity. Its locomotive is the least complex in steam — an 0-4-0
saddle tanker. The railroad itself is basic; three
miles of light iron which run from a textile mill
in Lando to the Seaboard junction and Edgmoor.
Above, on a rainy October day, the little Porter
shoves a cut of boxcars into the mill yard. She
was built in 1917, sports a faded number 5 on her
cab and a spark arrester on her stack. It seems
ironic that this sooty old kettle should be the last
steam engine to survive in South Carolina, years
after newer, vastly more sophisticated Atlantic
Coast Line 4-8-4's and Seaboard articulateds were
unhesitatingly condemned to the scrapper's torch.

OF QUESTIONABLE FORTITUDE

Hidden deep within the bayous of mid-Louisiana are a number of gravel pits whose mysterious little railroads, escaping both the recognition of the *Official Guide* and the scrutiny of the I.C.C., were long neglected. Then it was discovered that even as the victorious diesel hordes cleared practically all other steam power from the rails, steam locomotives, and odd ones at that, still hauled gondolas loaded with gravel around some of these pits. *At left,* a trim Baldwin 4-6-0, built in 1928 for something obviously more glamorous than a gravel yard, backed a hopper toward a train she was assembling. The one and a half miles of track which the ten-wheeler calls home, bears the impressive title of Washington and Western Railroad, and is owned by the Standard Gravel Co. Parked in the woods nearby were two Illinois Central 0-6-0's, a Mississippi Central 2-8-2, and a Southern Pacific 0-6-0. *At right* is a ghost of a locomotive which, although unfit for work, still sees plenty of use. Probably the oldest engine still in revenue service in the United States, the Willis Shortline's 4-6-0, No. 200, is, according to her crew, "at least 75 years old." There are no visible traces of who built her or when, but claims have been ventured dating her back to 1881. No. 200's crew has used much baling wire and friction tape to keep her running, and the leaking cylinder (*below*) is typical of the mechanical vicissitudes she has endured in recent years.

LAST OF THE NARROW GAUGES

The rapidity with which technology and war have accelerated the normal passage of time in the 20th century has tended to push the devices and events of decades just past into a kind of historical limbo. So it is with the steam locomotives which only recently aroused such intense rapture in the thoughts of the train watchers who knew their every habit. With the total disappearance of steam engines virtually an accomplished fact, the age of steam seems far behind indeed, rather than a time so recently departed.

One feels the closet kinship with the fascinating past when riding on rails which are spaced but three feet apart. For it was on this narrow-gauge trackage, mostly built during the 1870's and '80's, that so much of the ingredients of adventure and historical significance were blended to add to the store of intangibles that compose a people's heritage.* In the 1960's, only two steam-powered narrow-gauge lines remained in service in the United States and one in Mexico. The Denver & Rio Grande Western still ran revenue freight (usually two or three trains weekly) along a winding route which climbs over the continental divide and across the New Mexico-Colorado state line more than a dozen times. The East Broad Top ran a commendable passenger service through the beautiful Aughwick Valley in Pennsylvania during the Summer. These two roads, both 100 per cent steam-powered, comprise what little narrow-gauge trackage remained in use, except for the White Pass & Yukon, which runs from Skagway, Alaska to Whitehorse, in the Yukon. Only the Rio Grande was still in revenue service among the Continental U.S. narrow gauges, for the mines which comprised the EBT's main source of revenue closed down in 1956. Narrow-gauge railroads, two or three miles in length have been appearing all over the country in recent years, but these are all tourist attractions, usually built of salvaged equipment from abandoned roads and bear-

* See *Mixed Train Daily* by Lucius Beebe and Charles Clegg, E. P. Dutton & Company, Inc., New York. 1947.

ing little resemblance, in operation or location, to their original condition.

The virtues of narrow-gauge construction were demonstrated after the Civil War when it was found that such systems could often be built for half the cost of standard gauge, and were ideally suited for the hairpin curves and light axle-loadings of mountain railroading. The Rio Grande was built at an amazing pace during 1880 and 1881 by General William J. Palmer, a man whom Rio Grande men today say "must have thrown a glob of Spaghetti on a map of Colorado" to plan his route. Even today, the precarious shelves which support the frail trackage and send it over dainty bridges and through forgotten towns impress all who ride over them, and it seems inconceivable that men, mules and money were all that could be mustered to build the line in less than two years, when Indian raids were still a distinct possibility.

Once, over 2,000 miles of slim-gauge climbed, curved and somehow carried little trains all over the Colorado Rockies, reaching from Denver to Salt Lake City and rendering many a previous engineering "wonder" of the 19th Century an exercise in simplicity. This mileage was spread among a number of roads — the Rio Grande Southern, Colorado & Southern, Silverton Northern, to name a few. In the '60's only the D&RGW survived to celebrate an 80th anniversary, and its future was very much in the hands of the Interstate Commerce Commission which had repeatedly turned down Rio Grande abandonment petitions.

The rails to Telluride, Hesperus and Vanadium have vanished with the blizzards of yesteryear, but twenty foot drifts may still block

SUB-ZERO SPLENDOR

It is eight degrees below zero as No. 480, exhausting surplus steam from her cylinders, moves out to couple on to the train which she and helper 483 will haul over Cumbres Pass from Chama, New Mexico, to Alamosa; a day's journey eastward.

the three foot gauge to Farmington and completely close down the Silverton branch eight months each year.

The 1963 motive power roster of the Rio Grande narrow gauge consisted of 22 Mikados (seven of them unserviceable) of the 470, 480 and 490 classes. The rolling stock was chiefly comprised of hundreds of truss-rod boxcars, high gondolas, stock cars, flats, and a few steel framed tank cars and flats. The vast majority of the cars were of pre-1900 vintage, with minor modifications, and most rode on arch-bar trucks.

NARROW GAUGE SCENES

In addition to the rolling stock, there is much to interest railroad buffs on the D&RGW narrow gauge. *At left,* dampness seeping through a water tower has created a thick mantle of moss on the structure. During winter, huge cascades of ice reach to the ground from these tanks. *Below,* seven of the locomotives await heavy repairs or scrapping in the hoarfrost of a sub-zero January morning, while sister 483 shuffles by on her way to the snug roundhouse in Alamosa. *On facing page,* three 490 class K-37's await their assignments in the roundhouse on a warm June day.

COSTLY SNOW REMOVAL

Winter inevitably demands expensive non-revenue snow-removal trains over the 10,015-foot Cumbres Pass. Such a train was required the first week in January of 1963 when engines 484, 488, a snow spreader, a flanger and two cabooses cleared the line after a week of sporadic snow falls. The snow sometimes drifts over twenty feet at Cumbres, requiring a rotary plow pushed by three locomotives to clear the right of way. *Above,* the train starts around Cumbres Loop which, having been covered by only three feet of snow, took only ten minutes to clear. *Below,* the train paused briefly a few miles southwest of Antonito, on the edge of the San Luis Valley, where snow was negligible. Since each piece of equipment required locomotive steam for operation, the spreader was coupled behind the first engine, the flanger between the second engine and the cabooses. At *right,* the lead engine bites into 40 inches of new snow as she battles up the loop. The spreader then cleared the snow five feet back from the track, allowing ample clearance for the freight which was less than an hour behind. Once a train with only $400 revenue had to reach Farmington on schedule, resulting in a snow removal operation which required the rotary and cost the railroad $5,000!

TOURIST MECCA

Opposite: At the *upper left,* a snow train clears the tracks at Cumbres Pass. In the background, a snowshed covers the wye where the helper engines are turned. From here the track drops down a steady two per cent grade to Chama, the midway point on the Alamosa-Durango run. At the *lower left,* engine No. 473 moves up the canyon near Hermosa with nearly 400 passengers bound for Silverton. When the tourists began to discover the train, the railroad was somewhat surprised by the 12,000 passengers carried in 1953. That total had climbed to over 38,000 in the one hundred trips of the 1962 season, and showed no signs of abating. Since the line is maintained only four months a year, the Rio Grande is running what is probably the most profitable passenger train in the U.S. *Above,* a helper is cut into the middle of a freight on the east slope of Cumbres, and *below,* weight restrictions require that only one engine at a time cross the spindly Lobato Creek Trestle.

There is probably no other railroad in North America which boasts so much spectacular scenery in only 300 miles as the Rio Grande narrow gauge. It crosses level prairie and semi-desert, climbs to an altitude of nearly two miles, drops right down to the bed of the Animas River as it runs through the Canyon of the Lost Souls and passes scores of abandoned mines, decrepit towns of past glories, and Indian huts. Livestock still interferes with the loosely adhered-to schedules and the little Mikes haul their trains for many miles through territory completely void of any signs that the rugged frontier had indeed vanished, save for the undulating strip of rust that is the Rio Grande. Toltec Gorge is as breathless a spectacle as it was when Palmer's men passed it in 1880 and the terrain has experienced virtually no change since the Navajo hunters disappeared ninety years ago.

LONG FREIGHT

West of Gato a reasonably good road parallels
the track for miles and since the trains usually
travel under 30 mph it is relatively simple to pursue them by car and obtain many photos at each
passing. *Above,* just after coupling onto a train
of 55 cars pulled by engine 492, helper 491 leads
the way toward Durango. *Below,* the Navajo River
was nearly frozen as the pair of plucky Mikados
fought their way along its bank and up out of
the valley between Pagosa Junction and Arboles.

LAYOVER POINT

Freights heading west from Alamosa and east from
Durango usually meet at Chama where the crews
lay over for the night. *At right,* during a sub-zero
winter night two locomotives from the west-bound
freight and two from the snow train which pre-
ceded it, blow off steam while a fifth engine with
the east-bound freight in tow, arrives to silhouette
a caboose in its headlight beam. By 10 o'clock
the following morning the three trains had departed, leaving Chama in frigid slumber.

Perhaps the greatest irony in the lamentable affair which brings the most wonderful railroad network ever constructed to the brink of extinction is the inability of a potentially vastly powerful and resourceful railfan organization to put aside sectional jealousies and petty differences in order to save that which they profess to love so much. For example, a decade ago, a few dedicated groups pleaded in vain for aid in saving the Rio Grande Southern. The RGS went the way of virtually all narrow gauges and today those fans who would not give a dime, spend endless hours in somber contemplation of a roadbed denuded of wooden ties and steel rails. They cling to such remnants as spikes or switch stands when today they could cling to the grab irons of ten-wheeler No. 20 as the miners did in the boisterous days of great wealth and riotous living, when as many as twenty trains a day passed close under the eternal scrutiny of the barren peak known as Old Lizard Head and the riches of Colorado rode the express cars.

Compounding this unpleasant situation is the fact that what is probably the most fabulous line of all — the Rio Grande's branch to Silverton — is still in operation largely because of tourists. The people whom many railfans aloofly scorn as "daisy pickers" are the ones who, by filling the coaches to capacity through

"MUDHEN"

Above, when the famous Consolidations of the 1890's were due for replacement as principal freight power in 1903, fifteen 2-8-2's were built by Baldwin. Not handsome by most standards, these engines came to be known as "Mudhens." The last of them, No. 464, is spending its last days in the Durango yard. The publicity-conscious D&RGW dubbed the thirty Mikes built between 1923 and 1930 "sport models."

"SPORT MODEL"

At right, after a round trip to Silverton, engine No. 473 rides the Durango turntable. The term "sport model" must have gone to someone's head in the publicity department, for the Silverton engines have been made "touristy" by the addition of ridiculous phony diamond stacks, which in a vain attempt to give the 1923 Baldwins an 1890 look, only serve to accent the esthetic shortcomings of 473 and identical sisters 476 and 478.

the summers, have turned the 45-mile Silverton line into an activity which is rapidly becoming the biggest tourist attraction in Colorado. Indeed, the little 470-series Mikados often leave disappointed families on the Durango platform as they haul capacity trains of tourists for the six-hour daily round trip! In spite of the general apathy among many fans concerning "foreign-aid" — i.e. anything more than a few miles from home — the Silverton branch is probably safe, even when the remainder of the three-foot trackage will inevitably be ripped off the face of the Rockies.

The local economy is dependent on it to such a degree that Silverton and Durango fought the Rio Grande's abandonment attempts at every turn — another example of the "other guy" doing the railfan's job.

It was Lucius Beebe's books which first awakened the touring public to the wonders of the Silverton branch through Animas Canyon. What will it take to stir railfans out of mourning the passing of the steam locomotive long enough to save the largest concentration of them still operating in the United States — the Rio Grande narrow gauge?

"NARROW GAUGE CAPITAL"

Opposite, after a day's work, two engines take on coal at the tipple in Durango while another backs onto the turntable. Durango officially calls itself "the narrow gauge capital of the world," and the railroad is deeply engrained in the local economies of both Durango and Silverton. The railroad also maintains a large coaling stage at Chama and a lesser facility at Alamosa. Water towers are strategically placed at points along the system.

THREE-FOOT RAILROADING

Above, the conductor and head brakeman, after exchanging final information, return to their respective positions in a Farmington-bound freight, as snow begins falling. The railroad's chief source of revenue is well-drilling equipment and pipe such as that loaded on the gondolas above. *Below,* a crewman has gone forward to check if a nocturnal rockslide has left any sizable debris on the track. The obstructing rocks were quickly cleared.

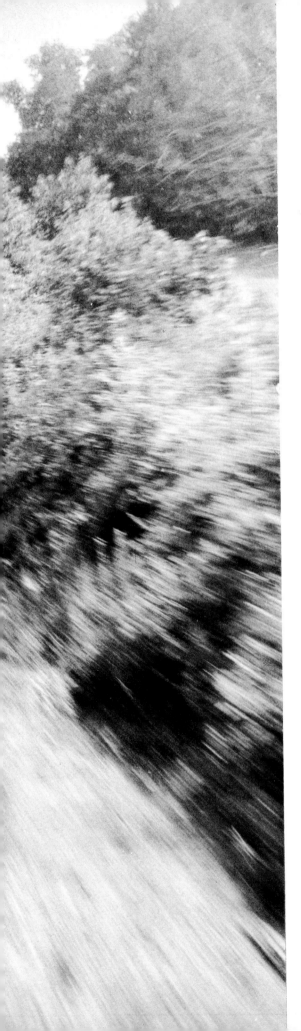

RESURRECTED GHOST IN PENNSYLVANIA

The East Broad Top Railroad, headquartered at Rockhill Furnace (Orbisonia), Pennsylvania is the only narrow gauge line east of the Mississippi still operating in its original location. It is just off U.S. Route 522, north of Exit 13 of the Pennsylvania Turnpike. During June, September and October, trains are run hourly on Saturdays and Sundays, beginning at noon. July and August find the three operational Mikados — Nos. 12, 14 and 15, running a daily schedule for the five-mile trip to Shirleysburg and return. A new wye has been built on the edge of a pleasant picnic grove near Shirleysburg. Picnickers may ride one train out to this area, and take any later train back.

Behind this wonderful operation is the fascinating story of the death and rebirth of a fine little railroad. The EBT was completed in 1874 and derived its principal revenue from coal until the market collapsed in 1955. The line was sold for scrap, but in 1960, owner Nick Kovalchick decided to start running trains over 3½ miles of the nearly 33 miles of track in operation at the time of abandonment. Enjoying early success, another one and a half miles were re-opened and the picnic area added. The whole line, though gathering rust and weeds, is still intact. Every car is in storage at Rockhill Furnace, and even the two standard gauge 0-6-0s which used to switch at the Pennsy junction in Mount Union are locked in a shed. Mikados Nos. 16 and 17 and a gas-electric are stored in the roundhouse at Rockhill Furnace and a trolly car has been renovated as an added attraction.

The rolling stock which comprises the regular trains include two rare and beautiful cars. No. 20, now named "Orbisonia," is an immaculately preserved parlor car which President Grover Cleveland is said to have occupied on his fishing trips in Maine. Coach No. 8 is probably the only 3-foot gauge car ever to run on roller-bearings.

To Nick Kovalchick and his sympathetic attitude toward a railroad deserving better than the torch, we can only say thanks, and wish the EBT a fate such as chose to grace the Silverton line.

NO. 15 IN ACTION

Photographed from the rear of the doodle-bug and traveling at the same speed, engine No. 15 rounds a curve near Shirleysburg.

NOT CAMERA-SHY

Above, No. 15 clears her cylinders in the yard. The photogenic Mikes are never short on steam when cameras are about. In the foreground is an old stub-switch from which the rail slang term "bend the iron" (throw a switch) originated. *Below,* an Independence Day train heads for home.

MEXICAN NARROW GAUGE

Since so many Americans are traveling to Mexico to see the very last of U.S.-built steam power on the eve of its final destruction, a few words should be said for the National Railways of Mexico three-foot gauge, 300 miles of which are in operation, including the heavily traveled Mexico City-Puebla line, via Cuautla. Most of the power is supplied by a fleet of Baldwin 2-8-0's built during the first quarter of this century. Their oversized headlights lend a "cute," indeed a comical, appearance to their squat forms as they trundle across streets and into factory yards in Mexico City. Mixed trains, passenger trains, and freight operations are all in evidence as is much second-hand equipment from U.S. narrow gauge lines — notably the Rio Grande. The photo of the ramshackle roundhouse (*above*) could well have been made in 1915, such is the antiquity of the line. *Below,* at dusk, a 2-8-0 scoots past two others in the Mexico City yards. If the remaining standard gauge steam tempts one to travel to Mexico, the narrow gauge should clinch the argument in favor of such a journey.

RAILFANS AND DAISYPICKERS

When a steam-powered special momentarily pauses at a small community in Pennsylvania — or Wyoming or Ontario — the townspeople are likely to be as interested in viewing the antics of the passengers as they are in seeing a genuine steam locomotive. What manner of people are these who buy tickets to nowhere in particular in order to ride behind a belching steam engine; who often pour out of the train to photograph it on some remote river bank or cow pasture? A steam excursion looks odd indeed, with shutterbugs leaning precariously out of windows, tape recorders absorbing the sweet noises of every piston stroke and clicking rail joint, and fans forsaking the comfort of reclining seats to stand in a wind-swept baggage car, as close to the engine as possible.

There is more — much more than meets the eye — to the approximately 100,000 Americans who are listed under the broad category of "railfans." At one end of this spectrum are the fascinated boys who never quite grew up. These are the ones to whom the public press pays the greatest attention; and although they are a minority among the *aficionados,* they are largely responsible for all fans being categorized under such labels as "railroad nut."

Some of these people attempt to steal any railroadiana not welded down, from crossing signs to engine bells. However, the vast majority of railfans are serious enthusiasts who, having discovered an interesting hobby, actively pursue it. They are scrupulous about seeking permission before entering railroad yards, about obeying safety rules and being tactful with railroad officials who may still regard their en-

FAN ENGINES, LARGE AND SMALL

Below: A 15″ gauge Cagney 4-4-0 steams around a circle of track at the Pine Creek Railroad on U.S. Route 9, north of Freehold, New Jersey. The principal motive power of this non-profit fan operated system is a 3-foot-gauge Shay from the Ely Thomas Lumber Co. A Porter Mogul was also being renovated and several other locomotives and cars are owned by the Pine Creek, which operates Sunday afternoons from April through November. *Opposite:* The moon rises over a Chicago & Northwestern 4-6-0 at the Mid-Continent Railway Museum in Hillsboro, Wisconsin, as she and an 0-4-0 switcher awaited the boiler inspector in June, 1962. The Railway Historical Society of Milwaukee, Inc. operated these trains over the scenic Hillsboro & Northeastern Railway.

NATIONAL RAILWAY HISTORICAL SOCIETY

The NRHS, formed in 1935, boasts over 2,600 members in 50 chapters scattered throughout the U.S., plus members in Canada and nine other countries. These chapters hold regular meetings, sponsor local trips to railroad shops and yards, go on excursions behind steam, diesel and electric power, and generally advance the interests of the railfan hobby. Some of them own locomotives or private Pullman observation cars. One of the most active in the NRHS, the Atlanta Chapter played host to the 1962 Annual Convention with an excursion behind the trim Savannah & Atlanta 4-6-2 at *right* which is stored, along with the Gainesville Midland Decapods at *lower right,* in Atlanta. *Below,* Chatahoochie Valley 2-8-0 No. 21 is also owned and operated by the NRHS.

thusiasm with some reservations. The railfan may belong to a local rail club or be affiliated with one of the national organizations. He contributes a valuable service to the preservation of historical data, equipment, and archives of American railroading. To this end, many railfan organizations have been responsible for maintaining railroad museums, displaying locomotives, and quite often, operating their own railroads. At the far end of the railfan spectrum are those whose love for railroads has been turned into employment, either part-time or full-time. Aside from the obvious cases of fans who actually become railroad men, there are those who write books, magazine and newspaper articles, sell photographs, and pub-

lish recordings of railroad sounds. The most famous railfan (although he disowns that pedestrian title) is Lucius Beebe, who has written many railroad books which have enjoyed widespread popularity.

Many railfans have become first-class historians. For just as the railroads' fortunes are inseparable from those of the nation, so are their histories. A railfan who can relate the early history of the Denver & Rio Grande Railroad can often paint an accurate verbal portrait of the carousing frontier life in Durango and Salida as well.

As may be expected among enthusiasts of anything having the vastness and complexities of railroading, there are a great number of specialists among fans. Certainly the steam buff is the most fanatical of them and heaven help the innocent passengers who may occupy seats near such an enthusiast when he encounters a diesel fan on an excursion. There are also electrification enthusiasts ("juice bugs"), especially the trolley fans who, like their beleagured compatriots in steam, are forever attempting to disprove the accusations leveled against their favorite motive power. For like the steam locomotive, the trolley cars' virtues were realized, it seems, only after the trolleys had been exterminated. Some fans specialize in passenger trains and equipment (another vast field) and others are more interested in the business practices and histories of the in-

dustry. Virtually every serious railfan has his own favorite railroad, and will devote much of his time to riding on it, walking along it, studying it, and writing about it. Some of these people become so expert that a railroad may often seek their advice when planning trips or writing histories. There are also model railroaders who will photograph and measure unusual freight cars, buildings and equipment and build beautiful scale models of them.

It is only within the past few years that the railroads have begun to realize the practical potential of people who, not owning stock or having railroad jobs, are genuinely interested in a business which has been the victim of incredible abuses from all levels of government and of public apathy. The railfans are willing to help the railroads, if the railroads will only let them.

PRIVATE HOBBY ENGINES

A few railfans own operational steam engines, two of which are shown here. The 0-4-2T (*above*) belongs to Henry L. Sorensen, of Arcata, California. He has done a superb job of restoring the 1908 Vulcan saddle-tanker after it had been rusting for years, buried in mud up to its smokebox. At *upper right,* Sorensen's teen-age son, Clifford, and daughter, Donna Kay, polish up No. 1 before a Sunday afternoon of running around the ranch. The strange caboose came from the Arcata & Mad River R.R. and was converted from a coach in 1931. Gus Haggmark, a friend of Sorensen, has built another caboose, from C&S narrow gauge plans. There is also a 1929 Baldwin 0-4-2T in the engine house, being renovated. At *right,* a side-tanker, the property of W. W. Willock Jr., on the trestle of his Indian Valley R.R. at Muttontown, Long Island. The railroad is being moved to a large farm near Chestertown, Maryland.

Opposite, at Clark's Trading Post, North Woodstock, New Hampshire, two woodburners, a Climax and a Heisler, operate during the Summer. Most of the visitors who come to see Ed Clark's performing bears probably do not realize that these two engines are virtually the last woodburners in service in the U.S., and there are few other Climaxes under steam, anywhere. Here the timeless chore of "wooding up" is being performed on the Heisler with the aid of a steam powered saw. At the *lower left,* a saddle tanker and a Heisler are parked on the right-of-way of the Puget Sound Railway Historical Association's track near Snoqualmie, Washington. The PSRHA owns nine locomotives, including an extremely rare 2-4-4-2 Mallet which, when it is restored by 1965, will probably be the only operating articulated locomotive in North America. *Below,* stored in the Santa Fe yards at San Bernardino, California, is the last S.P. 4-10-2 "Southern Pacific" type steam engine. It is owned by the Southern California Chapter of the Railway & Locomotive Historical Society, which hopes to run the big engine again. At *right,* similar to the small railroad at Disneyland, California, a steam engine hauls tourists and city children around Freedomland in the Bronx, New York.

The last sizable two-foot-gauge line in the United States is the Edaville Railroad at South Carver, Massachusetts. Built on a cranberry plantation, this 5½-mile railroad is all that remains of the lilliputian lines which once ran between the small communities in central Maine. There are several small 0-4-0T engines as well as coaches and freight cars. In an excellent state of preservation, the only 24-inch gauge parlor car ever built is displayed in one end of the museum. Also housed in this building are a large collection of tinplate and toy trains, scale models and other railroadiana, as well as an antique auto and fire engine collection. There is also a room full of Revolutionary War era Kentucky rifles. The Edaville chicken barbecue is good, and the tiny engines puff by right next to the picnic grove. There is also some standard gauge equipment on display and even a diesel, the Boston & Maine's "Flying Yankee" (*below background*), the first diesel streamliner in New England. The ride is quite pleasant, especially during the cranberry harvesting season, when the whole operation may be viewed from the passing trains, and the special runs around Christmas are known throughout New England.

WHITE PASS POWER IN DAKOTA

Up in the far northwest, one of the few common-carrier narrow gauges operating in the United States is the White Pass & Yukon, 110 miles of three-foot-gauge which winds from Skagway, Alaska, at sea level, up over the 2,885-foot White Pass, only twenty miles distant, through the upper reaches of British Columbia and across barren mountains to Whitehorse, capital of the Yukon Territory. Spawned by the Klondike gold rush in the closing years of the 19th Century, the WP&Y enjoyed a riotous early prosperity — much like its Colorado counterparts fifteen years previously. By 1920, the railroad was a pauper, and remained such until 1942, when the Japanese, skipping across the Aleutian Islands toward Alaska, cast the railroad in a new and immensely strategic role. The U.S. Army took over operations; brought up 26 narrow gauge engines from such varied sources as the D.&R.G.W., Denver, South Park & Pacific and the Eastern Tennessee & Western North Carolina; added them to an existing roster of 10 locomotives, and turned the WP&Y into a big time operation. There were several brand new 2-8-2's, hastily diverted to the Yukon in 1943, which later wound up on tourist roads in the U.S.

In 1945 WP&Y returned to its less hectic prewar existence (after having contrived to move 22 times more tonnage in 1943 than it did in 1935); and today the roar of steam is only an occasional treat on the White Pass & Yukon, for diesels have displaced the veterans of War in most of the railroad's work. At *right,* one of the largest WP&Y engines, No. 69, an outside-frame Consolidation fitted with a silly square headlight and fake diamond stack, now chuffs away all of her summers along a Burlington branchline in South Dakota, as Black Hills Central's "Klondike Casey." She runs on dual-gauge track through the Black Hills from Hill City to "Oblivion," five miles distant. An ex-Prescott & Northwestern (Arkansas) 2-6-2 also carries passengers on the standard gauge track.

TOURIST RAILROADS IN THE SOUTHWEST

California, known for its attractions to delight tourists, abounds in playhouse railroading ventures, some of which are mentioned elsewhere in this volume. One place which has a more genuine quality of the real old West about it is Knott's Berry Farm, whose proprietors actually brought dilapidated structures in off the desert to create a memorable and educational 1890 atmosphere. Here is some vintage Rio Grande narrow gauge equipment which, if one ignores the gaudy paint, should prove of great interest to narrow gauge enthusiasts. Aside from the locomotive at the Colorado Railroad Museum (page 69) the two 2-8-0's at Knott's Berry Farm are the only 19th century Colorado three-footers still active. *Above,* one of them, No. 40, rounds a curve, passing some of the antiquities of Old California which are scattered about the property. At *left,* an air of mystery surrounds the future of the narrow gauge Heisler which shared an engine house with a Mogul, a 4-6-0, and an 0-4-0T in Roseville, California. This equipment, operating as the Antelope & Western in 1962, was part of an alleged collection of 20 operational narrow gauge locomotives for which big plans were reportedly being made.

VALHALLA OF THE DAISYPICKER

In railfan vernacular a "daisypicker" ("berry-picker" in Canada) is a tourist or other non-railfan who is apt to be off in the fields admiring nature instead of the 4-8-4 which the fans are busily photographing. One daisypicker's delight is the Rebel Railroad at Pigeon Forge, Tennessee. There is an applied Western atmosphere (way east in the Smoky Mountains) and the rolling stock sparkles with gaudiness. The fake diamond stack on the ex-White Pass & Yukon 2-8-2 may be understandable, but the extremely poor taste used in painting the two locomotives at *right* makes steam fans cringe. There is no effort here to preserve steam as it was. In spite of its faults however, the Rebel Railroad is live steam and worth visiting. *Above,* in the dead of Winter, the Rebel sleeps. The fans should not forget that the daisypickers are the primary reason why many steam engines are still operating.

"TWEETSIE, THE BEAUTIFUL NARROW GAUGE"

There was, in bygone years, a small railroad which meandered barely a few miles either side of the state line between Tennessee and North Carolina. The East Tennessee & Western North Carolina was, to quote Lucius Beebe's chronology of little railroads, *Mixed Train Daily,* "the beautiful narrow gauge." From its beginning in 1882, the ET&WNC had become the beloved possession of the folk who inhabited the splendid countryside up around Grandfather Mountain. To them, pleasant little ten-wheelers on the three-foot-gauge track were known by the affectionate name of "Tweetsie." For years Tweetsie was their vital link with the outside world, but the encroachments of internal combustion on paved roads upset the delicate economic balance which had meant life or death to the frail line. Tweetsie, like its western cousin, the Rio Grande Southern, was not immune to the adversities of nature and their ensuing expense.

When floods caused the abandonment of half of Tweetsie's mileage and ended passenger service entirely in 1940, Miss Annette Vance, a resident of Minneapolis, North Carolina, spoke for many of the railroad's friends when she wrote a poem of remorse in the simple direct manner of the mountain folk. A few lines from it are:

> *"When she passed, we stood amazed,*
> *We admired her so we stood and gazed.*
> *Her loss we pine, we loved her so . . ."*

The last line was the now oft-repeated plea which became synonomous with Tweetsie's demise:

> *"Please send us back our little train."*

The brief flurry of business brought on by the War could not save Tweetsie and she quietly died in 1951, leaving only the standard gauge portion of the ET&WNC (page 102) which remained one of the last bastions of steam well into the 1960's. The memories of

Tweetsie were long to remain, however, and some of the property was saved; including what is probably the most famous 4-6-0 in the U.S.; Tweetsie No.12. So it was, that Tweetsie was to be resurrected — in a grotesque form, to be sure — but nevertheless, North Carolina has regained its "little train." No.12, aided by another second-hand White Pass & Yukon engine, resplendent in tourist livery (*above*) now runs circles around a mountain near Blowing Rock, North Carolina. The new Tweetsie Rail-road is a gaudy side show complete with the usual cowboys (*opposite page*), indians, flashy paint and other characteristics of tourist places which cater to the Brownie camera set. Tweet-sie's old friends may still ride behind No. 12, but they must wonder if indeed their little train is not really a ghost beyond recall.

JOURNEY TO YESTERDAY

The railfan hobby came into its own during the late 1930's. It was then that railfan periodicals (including several for model builders) made an appearance, the National Railway Historical Society was formed, the first hardcover books of railroad photography were published and people began to charter trains to nowhere in particular — just for the sheer joy of riding behind a locomotive.

The postwar decline of the steam engine turned the nature of these rail excursions from small fan trips involving three or four cars into gala affairs which may utilize double-headed Northerns and twenty-two coaches. In the 1960's the only chance of riding behind steam is on such a special, resulting in most active fan groups sponsoring at least an occasional such venture.

The Illini Railroad Club, headquartered at Champaign, Illinois, probably promotes more rail specials than any other organization, and they are usually interesting and well-planned;

two virtues sometimes lacking in otherwise well-meaning railfan enterprises. Perhaps the successes of the Illini Club may be attributed to the fact that its president, M. H. Klebolt, is a full-time planner and supervisor of rail tours. Maury Klebolt and the "Chief Illini" — an open-platform Pullman observation car — have roamed the nation behind steam and diesel power.

The most spectacular undertaking in the Illini itinerary is the late Spring "Journey To Yesterday"; an annual pilgrimage to that great shrine of steam, the narrow gauge division of the Denver & Rio Grande Western Railroad in Colorado. This week-long 3,000 mile round trip from Chicago to Alamosa and the entire narrow gauge trackage still operating as a common-carrier in the United States, utilizes steam power of three or four railroads and a minimum of diesel power. These pages record the "Journey" of June 2-9, 1962; a trip which could be made for as little as $200, including all rail fares, three nights lodging in Alamosa, and almost half of the meals.

The railfans had gathered at gate 16 of Union Station in Chicago on June second. Luggage and photography equipment were

RECORDING STEAM

Above: Most fan trips are provided with 120-volt power outlets in the baggage car, enabling tape recorders to be used. While fans hold their microphones, Brad Miller of Mobile Fidelity Records tends to his elaborate equipment in the foreground. Much of MF's "Sunday Only" album was recorded on this trip. *Below:* 5632 crosses the Mississippi River, bound for Burlington, Iowa.

stacked high near the entrance and grand expectation excited the conversations of the anxious group of steam seekers. When at last the gate opened, many of the fans hastily deposited their belongings at their assigned seats and rushed to the head of the train where the big and formidable Chicago, Burlington & Quincy 4-8-4, No. 5632, was engaged in challenging diesel supremacy with all manner of hellish noises and fiery epithets hurled as if in vengeance. Her place was clear as the very last defender of main-line steam on the Burlington, and she never ceased playing the role for her admirers.

At the last moment, several passengers who

WATERING COLUMN

Left: Although the C.B.&Q. has removed many of its watering facilities, some remain, such as this column at New London, Iowa. Since it had not been used since the previous time 5632 came through, in 1961, the fireman had to let it run for several minutes to clear algae out of the water. The boiler of a locomotive is sensitive to impurities, so the railroad adage "if you wouldn't drink it, don't put it in an engine" still applies. *Below:* Passengers in the dome of the coach, and at *right,* 5632's nocturnal arrival at Creston, Iowa.

had been on hand at the awakening of the prima donna at Clyde Roundhouse hours before, boarded the train and the famed Northern commenced a gala performance which was to continue to Lincoln, Nebraska, 500 miles westward.

There was much roaring and belching of smoke as 5632, after halting to allow fans to disembark, backed up a few thousand feet, and came thundering back for the benefit of tape recorders and cameras. Of the photo runs made that day, the one across the Mississippi River was the most spectacular.

It would not be exaggeration to estimate that 5,000 people came to see 5632 as she sped across the prairie, at times nearing 100 miles per hour. If Illinois had become somewhat accustomed to the busy Northern's nomadic wanderings, Iowa and eastern Nebraska, which see steam only once or twice annually, went wild over the appearance of 5632. Anyone who rode the train that day could not help but feel the deep ties between the great locomotive and the big story of America. It was all there; the frightened horses galloping to the far pasture fence; the motorists waving at every

LOCOMOTIVE AND LIVESTOCK

The way livestock interfered with the urgent progress of the iron horse was often evident on this trip. Once the train was delayed while Indian shepherds drove 300 head of sheep across the right-of-way. A magnificent black stallion, with white mane and tail shimmering in the setting sun, had been feeding on the track as the aggressive Mike rounded a curve. The horse, closely pursued by the locomotive, galloped up the track and disappeared into the hills. The motion of animal and machine was poetic. After dark, as the train neared Durango, the headlight beam spotted an old cow, walking unconcernedly between the rails.

She yielded the track long enough to give the engineer clearance, then true to her bovine nature, she repossessed the track a few seconds ahead of the locomotive. However, the cowcatcher is still a functional device and when last seen, the foolish cow was running across the pasture, bellowing as she vanished into a ravine, stampeding the other cattle in the field. All of the local dogs delight in chasing the trains off their domains and seem quite proud of their calling. *Above,* Richard A. James of Colton, California, resplendent in his railroad shirt, tries for a new angle with his camera. *Below:* Fans photographing a 70-car freight which met the Illini special at Cumbres Loop.

grade crossing; the photographers on virtually every bridge; the humor of a tourist with Massachusetts license plates driving straight into a ditch as his startled family gaped at a venerable 238-ton black ghost puffing across their path. At water stops, the townspeople (often forewarned by newspaper articles) came to see the Northern quench her great thirst (sometimes with the help of local fire departments), while automobiles and bicycles converged upon the scene from surrounding farmlands. There were instances when 5632 was enveloped in crowds of a density that required several whistle blasts to clear the right of way. That night a group gathered in a darkened vista-dome, and with the steady beat of 5632's exhaust for accompaniment, sang new lyrics to "Springtime in the Rockies";

> "...narrow gauge, you are my sweetheart,
> with your rails three feet apart."

The finest performance given by 5632 was one witnessed by only a dozen fans in the baggage car long after sunset. After crossing the Missouri River, the engine encountered a steep grade leading up to Nebraska City. It had been raining and the driving wheels slipped on the wet rails. Like most oil-burners, the struggling locomotive shot flicking jets of flame out from her firebox. Her exhaust, which is normally deafening, became almost unbearable in the baggage car, as it echoed off the rock wall of the cut. The engine crew must have sensed the grandeur of the moment, for the whistle was screaming continually as the sharp light of the firebox illuminated the glistening rocks. When the summit was finally attained amid a crescendo of smoke and noise and swirling vapors, townspeople were standing in the drizzle; visible for a moment in the sweeping head-

SILVERTON SMOKE

The fabled Silverton train was a highlight of the itinerary and the Illini fans were among the first of the 1962 season to make the trip. Thirty-eight thousand tourists and fans followed during the next three months. Here the homely No. 473 with conspicuous airpumps characteristic of her class, lays down the soot to the satisfaction of the shutterbugs on the maintenance-of-way cars.

NO. 487 SHOWS OFF

Above: On the first photo run of the trip to Farmington, New Mexico, No. 487 turned in a laudable performance while crossing the trestle near Carbon Junction. The boxcar carried the fan's baggage and stayed with the train throughout the trip. *Below:* One of the last trains to traverse the old line near the new Navajo Dam, the Illini Special is crossing the middle of a valley destined to become a huge lake. The line relocation actually added four miles to the narrow gauge trackage — a happy reversal of the prevailing trend.

light beam. As the victorious Northern strutted past, they cheered her coming. In town, porch lights suddenly flicked on as families abandoned their cozy homes to see the show, thrilled at the visitor from a bygone era. The whole spectacle left those in the baggage car speechless. Later attempts (such as this writing) to convey the emotions of the experience failed to do it justice.

The 5632 departed at Lincoln, where she was to run shorter excursions until the return of the Illini extra from Colorado. A diesel ran the sleeping fans to Denver by morning, then a diesel-powered trip was made over the two famous scenic routes of the Denver & Rio Grande Western — the Moffat Tunnel and the Royal Gorge. Leaving Pueblo after midnight, the train reached Alamosa next morning. A Rio Grande narrow gauge Mikado, No. 483, coupled on to her train, composed of all of the serviceable narrow gauge passenger equipment, plus a reconditioned gondola, and headed into the wildly beautiful Rocky Mountain scenery which lay south and west — toward Durango.

Then followed four days of ceaseless wonders as the excursion train wound its way all over the remaining narrow gauge trackage in Colorado and New Mexico. With Durango as the junction point, trips were made to Farmington and Silverton on successive days. After 600 miles of narrow gauge travel, the sooty fans returned to their standard gauge cars in Alamosa.

HELPER GIVES A BOOST

The fourth day on the narrow gauge saw the fans returning to their standard gauge connection at Alamosa. At *right,* a helper was employed to return the train to the summit of Cumbres Pass. Although summer was well along in the Rockies, snow was still visible on the reverse slopes.

The fans did not realize that the famous Consolidation which the Colorado & Southern had sent to Denver Union Station to pull the special north to Fort Collins on June eighth was only months from retirement. She proudly wheeled out ahead of the sleek California Zephyr which had occupied the adjoining track. *Above,* the 638 pauses briefly at Boulder, Colorado, which at the moment was too excited by the homecoming of her distinguished son, astronaut Scott Carpenter, to pay much attention to the 2-8-0. The star of the day however, was that inimitable sugar beet-hauling Decapod, Great Western's No. 90. This 1924 Baldwin, probably the last 2-10-0 under steam in the United States, continued to amass scores of admirers and in the 1960's reference to "The Decapod" in railfan circles meant No. 90; no elaboration was necessary. On the facing page, she has just taken the train from the C&S engine which is turning on the wye. The 638 ran light southbound, later returning the train to Denver. *Below,* the fans line up to capture the smoky antics of No. 90 on film. Habitually erupting sparks, these locomotives occasionally set the adjoining prairies to merry blazes. In a few dry areas the Illini special swept by in a literal blaze of glory.

A RIDE IN THE CAB

After five days of traveling behind the last of Colorado's narrow and standard gauge steam, the familiar 5632 again took up her position at the head end. There were the usual stops for photo runs, and more often than not, the Burlington had to contact the local fire departments of one-line communities to send pumpers to fill the 4-8-4's tank; for most watering facilities had long since been dismantled. Many people familiar with steam locomotives during their prime had declared the Burlington 5600's among the noisiest.

A ride in 5632's cab dispels any doubt of the validity of that theory. A visitor occupies the head brakeman's seat, immediately behind the fireman. The engineer, after giving two deafening blasts on the whistle (which had been salvaged from a scrapped M-4) eases out the throttle and the 0-5 lurches forward for a 45-minute run across the Iowa prairie, a run which seldom touches speeds under 70 mph. The spacious cab is hot and the deck plate clangs incessantly against the tender. The engineer and fireman have to shout their signals across the seven feet of backhead which separates their seats. The noise is ear-piercing, with exhaust, blowers, whistle, and running-gear competing for supremacy. Compound this with a hundred creaking, squealing, crashing metal surfaces, and you cannot help but feel the madness of a 238-ton boiler hurtling un-

BURLINGTON SPLENDOR

Here, 5632 performs for her admirers, some of which seek unique camera angles from a signal. The photo *above* was made by suspending the camera beneath the cab and using a delay-action shutter. At *left,* while the tender is being filled by the local fire department, the townspeople of Chariton, Iowa, have come to see the big Northern halted conspicuously across a main thoroughfare. The "Journey to Yesterday" is a long trip (one week, 3,000 miles), but there are some even more elaborate, including tours of Latin-American or European railroads, perhaps totaling 10,000 miles in several weeks, sponsored by various groups around the nation.

177

checked toward seemingly inevitable destruction. You remember all too clearly that a mere lip of metal flange on each wheel is all that prevents this belching monster from careening down the next embankment.

The presence of super power is everywhere; in the momentum and the resounding crescendo of steam and steel, leaving you stunned with a sensation of having saddled a meteor, angering some vengeful deity in the process of the transgression. The shock of meeting a westbound express on the adjoining track at a passing speed of 170 mph, veers the engine toward the right. A brief instant of increased clatter marks the passing of a manifest freight. The speedometer needle sways between 85 and 90 mph as the brakeman pours a cup of coffee. In your unaccustomed hand, the cup is emptied before it can reach your mouth; so great is the vibration.

A sudden lurch when your guard is down throws you against a bulkhead. You wonder that men can spend so much of their lives in the heat and violence of a cubicle which offers only an endless array of valves, levers and switches, of flames, pandemonium — and always — formidable adventure.

While the 5632 sped toward Chicago, Maury Klebolt chatted with his guests, including two British railroad men, John Baldwin and Raymond Ruffell, in the "Chief Illini." The Englishmen had made their first trip to the U.S. especially for this excursion, and had a "jolly good" time. They took warm memories back to England, and later received many gifts from their U.S. railfan acquaintances.

EXCURSION ENGINES OF THE '60's

Since active steam power was completely banished from revenue service on Class One railroads by 1960, the few locomotives which prudent railroad officials saved for special trips were bound to achieve widespread recognition. The Burlington had run steam extras since shortly after dieselization in 1955, when the big O-5's were in stand-by service. As long ago as 1948, Union Pacific's now famous No. 844 was assigned to fan trips, and the Canadian National has always cooperated with fans and other interested parties who sought the thrills of steam railroading for perhaps the last time. Most railroads ran specials in the last days of steam, but it was to the management of those roads which have kept steam operating into the 1960's, that the credit, and the rewards of customer goodwill go for taking a calculated business risk which has not been disappointing. Beginning with the Reading 2100's, reactivated in October 1959, the following pages chronicle the most important of these locomotives, most of which were but anonymous stereotypes of thirty, fifty, or even two hundred identical sisters, but a few years ago. These sisters have known the scrapper's torch and are gone, but the few survivors keep the memories fresh and vibrant.

READING 2100's

For two years the Reading Company's No. 2124 pulled the early "Iron Horse Rambles," sometimes coupled to sister 2100. When 2124 was retired, 2102 took her place. The other two remaining T-1's are the 2101, which is serviceable, and the 2123, being stripped for spare parts. At *left,* 2102 leaves Bethlehem, Pa., on a chilly morning. *Opposite,* 2100 leads 2102 and sixteen coaches along the bank of the Schuylkill River on the very popular "Autumn Leaves Ramble" of October 14, 1962.

BURLINGTON'S FINEST

Big and beautiful, the 35 4-8-4's which the Chicago, Burlington & Quincy had built between 1930 and 1940, were the finest locomotives on one of America's finest railroads. The "Q," as the Burlington's admirers refer to the railroad, saved two of these splendid engines. The 5629 serves as a temporary boiler whenever needed, and the 5632 has become a legend among railfans. She still romps with 10 steel cars at 100 mph, as she did in the days when she kept the famed Zephyrs to schedule, and nuzzling the speed limits is her cherished pastime. *Above,* after taking on water

at Creston, Iowa, the 5632 is ready for another division as sheets of rain envelope her in the regal splendor of wisping steam and elusive halos. (A comparison with the photo on page 85 will illustrate the fate which, but for a considerate Burlington management, may have overcome the 5632). The photo at *right* was made from the cab of the big Northern at 88 mph, as she wheeled an Illini excursion toward Colorado. The camera was on a six-foot tripod, hand-held, and extended from the cab. The exposure was 1/100 at F-8 on Plus-X film.

THE SPLENDOR OF STEAM IN ECHO CANYON

Certainly classics among Northerns, the 45 4-8-4's which the Union Pacific ran on its crack varnish and hot-shot freights deserved the acclaim lavished upon them. These 800's kept well the tradition of superpower maintained by their contemporaries; the Big Boy, Challenger and 4-12-2 "Union Pacific" types. The one fault of the 800's was the tendency of their drivers to slip when first starting; but once under way, they were second to none. The U.P. chose to honor its superb steam roster by saving the 844, last of the magnificent 4-8-4's. Although she now sees service only several days each year, her fame is equal to that of the busier Reading and Burlington engines. *Opposite,* the 844 (renumbered 8444 in 1962 to allow new diesels the 800 series classification) emerges from a tunnel near Uintah, a few miles east of Ogden. It was Labor Day and she was wheeling a Pacific Railroad Society special to Cheyenne. *Above,* the 844 blasts upgrade in Echo Canyon, where her bark and her whistle amply justified the name of that beautiful place. *Below,* for hundreds of miles, railfans and local residents paced the great engine. The Union Pacific plans to save the 844 for "intermittent service."

When the Canadian National Railways needed a universal locomotive to help solve the problems created by the great diversification of motive power, they turned to the brand-new 4-8-4 wheel arrangement in 1927. This decision was never regretted, for when the CNR finally stopped ordering Northerns, over 200 of them dominated the rosters of CNR and its U.S. subsidiary, Grand Trunk Western. Although small by U.S. standards, the U-series CNR 4-8-4's looked large and formidable; many being equipped with menacing feedwater heaters on their brows, large smoke deflectors, or other variations which were bound to permeate the ranks of so ubiquitous a roster of engines. The most famous of these Northerns turned out to be No. 6167. Typical of her type, this U-2-e weighed just over 200 tons, and her length, including the Vanderbilt-type tender, was only 91 feet, 4 inches (compared to the Reading's T-1's, whose engine weight is over 220 tons and whose huge tenders give them a length of 110 feet).

By 1962, Canadian National had only three serviceable steam engines; all slated for retirement by October. Pacific No. 5107 and Northern No. 6153 were retired after several successful double-headed fan trips. The latter engine went to the Canadian Railroad Historical Association museum at Dolson, Quebec. The 6167 received a one-year extension, however, but after October 1963 she faced the scrapper's torch, and steam, except for a very few industrial and short line engines, had left Canadian rails — probably forever.

BLIZZARD, SUB-ZERO AND THE 6167

Living on borrowed time, the last of Canadian steam howled her defiance in the grand manner as she pulled an over-loaded train of her faithful friends from Toronto to Orilia, around Lake Simcoe and back to Toronto — 190 miles. This journey, on January 27th 1963, was sponsored by the Upper Canada Railway Society; a dynamic group whose busy schedule was largely responsible for 6167's latter-day leases on life. *Above,* just north of Gormley, 6167 roars out of a snow storm and her own exhaust to the delight of fans in the deep Canadian Winter. *Above, left,* during a "run-past," as Canadians refer to photo stops, the 4-8-4 whips past Hawkestone Station at 60 mph. Canadians take these run-pasts quite seriously and conduct them in an excellent manner. *Below,* an icy wind and sub-zero temperatures combine to create a final scene of steam and snow at Barrie, on the edge of Lake Simcoe.

COZY AND FRIENDLY: THE STRASBURG

The four and one-half mile Strasburg Rail Road which meanders from Paradise to Strasburg, in the renowned Pennsylvania-Dutch county of Lancaster, Pa., is unique in many respects. First of all, the Strasburg is the oldest short-line railroad in America, having been chartered in 1832. Then, it was the first instance of a railroad being bought by railfans and operated successfully as a common-carrier. And, most unusual of all, the Strasburg Rail Road is on the way to becoming one hundred per cent steam powered! By 1958, declining business had left the Strasburg in a deplorable, indeed decadent, state. The track was rotting, the motive power, one gasoline mechanical engine, was in need of major repairs, and the railroad was on the verge of abandonment. Then a group of resourceful railfans bought the railroad, tackled the monumental task of restoration with more hope and muscle than money or equipment, and within three years had the finest, most pleasant little operation going; one which actually began to show promise of eventually paying for itself. The Strasburg's return to steam power (after 34 years of the gasoline engine) occurred with the purchase of one of those affable little Canadian National 0-6-0's, No. 7312. She soon became Strasburg No. 31, and began hauling passengers by the Labor Day weekend of 1960. After that, as the 55 year old shifter climbed to the national prominence of a color spread in *Life* magazine and a major tourist attraction, other steamers arrived on the property. Two were 4-4-0's; one loaned by the Pennsylvania. One of the most interesting was the last operating Camelback; an ex-Reading 0-4-0, bought from the Colorado Fuel & Iron Company, of Birdsboro, Pa. She has been assigned to switching duties at the East Strasburg yard. At *left,* symbolic of the downfall of steam, No. 31 puffs toward the oldest cemetery in Lancaster County. *Above,* the Strasburg station. In addition to the Amish countryside, the Strasburg boasts an on-line picnic area, a collection of 19th century passenger equipment on loan from the Pennsy, and one of the friendliest group of fellows who ever ran a railroad. Truly, the Strasburg is "the Road to Paradise."

MAINTENANCE ON THE GREAT WESTERN
Below: In Colorado, the Great Western's sugar beet and fan hauling Decapod, No. 90, pauses briefly while her fireman makes adjustments on the running gear.

THE GREAT TEACHER; NO. 4960

The Burlington wisely saved two locomotives of distinctly different types, which adds variety to their steam trips. While Northern No. 5632 may lead a nomadic existence over the entire railroad, Mikado No. 4960 is known more for jouncy little excursions out of Aurora, Illinois, and down the Fox River Valley to Ottawa, as on these pages. She has given thousands of children their first taste of steam (and perhaps, their last) in a rail-road educational program operated in cooperation with on-line school districts. Although, a homely and sooty coal hauler by profession, 4960 is deceptive; her 64 inch drivers often contriving to pass the mile-a-minute mark. In spite of her 40 years, the 2-8-2 is kept in top condition through the "steam preservation fund" — a wise practice of charging one dollar per passenger above the regular fare to ensure the finances to keep Burlington steam in service indefinitely.

In addition to the major railroads which have operated steam well into the 1960s, several smaller roads have retained locomotives for this purpose. Others, such as the Strasburg and the Arcade & Attica, bought steam power long after dieselization and now realize a good return on their investments as vacationers and railfans make the pilgrimage to ride the steam cars once more. Some Class One roads, realizing the folly of having junked all their steam power, may actively seek a locomotive to operate. Such was the case of the Long Island Rail Road, which was negotiating with a fan group to run their locomotive. Railfan organizations and individuals also own operable steam locomotives, and in time these too may acquire the fame now reserved for the locomotives in this chapter, and some of those, such as the East Broad Top, the Rio Grande, and the various operating museums, whose habits are reviewed elsewhere in this volume.

MOVIE RAILROAD

For several decades, the Sierra Railroad, headquartered at Jamestown, California, has provided steam power and a scenic right-of-way for Hollywood producers. Now diesels perform the revenue tasks, and two locomotives, an 1891 Rogers 4-6-0 and a 1922 Baldwin 2-8-0, are stored for movie chores and an occasional fan trip. At *right,* these two engines are seen in the roundhouse at Jamestown. Also in the house at the time (September 1962); two Mikados which were destined for a new steam operation in Arizona.

WANING GLORY

Above: The Colorado and Southern's 2-8-0 No. 638; among the last of that Burlington subsidiary's steam engines, runs through the sugar beet fields of northern Colorado in 1962, just before her retirement. At *left,* an Alco ten-wheeler, No. 94 of the Western Pacific, as she stood in the roundhouse at Oakland, California. Reputedly the last operable steam locomotive owned by the W.P., No. 94 is fired up on occasion for special events. *Below:* Minus her headlight but not her dignity, the queen of all fan-trippers, Reading T-1 No. 2124, her firebox forever cold, awaited final disposition in the roundhouse at Reading, Pa., in May 1962. It was the 2124, built at Reading's own shops in 1947, which powered the original "Iron Horse Rambles," starred in the opening scene of the film "From The Terrace" and was featured in a double page advertisement in national magazines, as well as two full page color spreads in a *Life* article. Her final home: permanent display at Steamtown, New Hampshire.

THE CONTINUING MOTIVE POWER DEBATE

By 1960 the general public and most rail-fans had come to accept the idea, repeated by diesel locomotive manufacturers and railroad motive power departments, that the steam locomotive was technologically obsolete, an anachronism held over from the 19th century. Then H. F. Brown, Ph.B., Fellow of the American Institute of Electrical Engineers and a railroad man since 1910, presented a paper entitled "Economic Results of Diesel Electric Motive Power on the Railways of the United States of America," before a meeting of the Institution of Mechanical Engineers in London in November of 1960. This skillfully researched paper attacking the arguments of the defenders of the diesel may prove to be quite an enlightening experience to those interested in railroad motive power economics as it becomes more widely circulated.*

To put it bluntly, Mr. Brown contends, the American railroads fell for a well planned sales campaign — and fell hard! Beginning in 1946, a number of U.S. railroads began a series of tests — pitting modern steam power against new diesels. These tests were well programmed, executed under controlled conditions, and closely chronicled in a thick volume entitled "Study of Railroad Motive Power," (File No. 66-A-11. Statement No. 5025) published by the Bureau of Transport Economics and Statistics of the Interstate Commerce Commission in May 1950.** Perhaps the most famous of these tests was the New York Central's series which set 4-8-4 Niagaras against diesels. The steam engines performed beyond expectations, some averaging nearly 30,000 miles a month and conceding little to the diesels. Years later, Norfolk & Western's superb Y-6b's were to run diesel demonstrators off the property in overall performance. Nickel Plate's Berkshires operating costs showed a "paper thin" difference compared with the diesels, and the diesel's claim to long-run superiority had long since been demolished by an oil-fired Santa Fe 4-6-4 which had made the 2,200 mile-plus trip from Chicago to Los Angeles in December 1938, without replacement.

* As long ago as 1943, Lucius Beebe, in his book *High Iron*, (D. Appleton-Century Company, Inc., New York), recognized the very essence of this diesel-steam controversy and wrote of it on pp. 156-159.
** This study, issued as information, was not considered or adopted by the I.C.C.

How, then, did the diesel locomotive manage to completely annihilate steam from Class-One revenue service within fifteen years after the latter was still performing 90% of all railroad work? First of all, the I.C.C. study was accepted at face value by many operating departments. This study was based largely on new diesels performing against modern, but war-weary, steam locomotives, usually under ideal conditions for the diesel — fast schedules, through freights, etc. The statistics were projected to diesels having a service life of 20 years (in 1950, only a few dozen early yard diesels had been in existence for 20 years), and steam locomotives having a life of 30 years. A decade later, virtually all diesels were being retired after only 12 to 14 years service, while a number of steam locomotives over 40 years old were still puffing about their daily work. The earliest use of diesel locomotives was in yard service, where they did show a substantial saving over existing steam power. It may be noted that Mr. Brown's findings were based on I.C.C. statistics which by 1960 had invalidated much of the 1950 report.

According to Mr. Brown, his paper was not intended to prove the superiority of one form of motive over another, but "simply to explore the fantastic economic claims which had been made for diesels." Those claims and Mr. Brown's findings follow:

1. "Each diesel had replaced two steam locomotives, and could do the work formerly performed by two steam locomoties." Perhaps; if the steamers happen to be 1905-vintage Moguls. The fact is that a 1,500 horsepower diesel unit never could out-perform a modern steam engine. It would take 2.41 diesel units to equal one 3,650 horsepower steam engine (the average modern steamer). Today as many as five diesel units are required to pull trains formerly requiring one 4-8-4!

2. "Diesels, by multiple unit operation, had enabled the railways to reduce the number of trains, by their ability to haul longer trains." Train lengths have changed little since World War II. The reduction in numbers of trains corresponds to the reduction in branch line and local freight, and in all passenger business.

3. "They were responsible for large savings made in wages of train and engine crews, due

to the reduction in number of trains operated." No credit due the diesel here; same as above. The railroads maintain that the diesel turned firemen into "featherbedders" in yard and freight service. This is the basis for a large amount of the present controversy between the brotherhoods and management.

4. "They had greatly increased the speed of trains." The U.S. speed records are still held by 4-4-0's, 4-4-2's and 4-6-2's. The *20th Century Limited* still takes 16 hours on the run from New York to Chicago; as when the Hudsons were on the head-end. Modern steam locomotives wheeled freight at 60 mph — comparable to present fastest runs. Schedules on some commuter runs had to be *lengthened* after diesels had bumped forty-year-old K-4's off the Pennsylvania's lines, because of the superior acceleration of the old 4-6-2's.

5. "They were responsible for a great reduction in locomotive repair costs." Elaborate filter systems, multiplicity of internal reciprocating parts, operating under high temperatures and pressures, expensive new facilities, and highly payed technicians show this to be a fallacy. (When the author visited the shops of the Lake Superior & Ishpeming Railroad in Marquette, Michigan, he found one of the two serviceable steam locomotives switching in the yard. A roundhouse man pointed to a stripped diesel chassis, saying: "It's been laid up for days awaiting a new part. In the old days we could have sent a man with a hammer and a piece of iron into the blacksmith shop, and a half hour later it would have been fixed.") Expensive replacement parts are another diesel maintenance factor.

6. "They had enabled the railways to make operating savings of up to 30 per cent annually, in the investment made in them after interest and depreciation charges, or enough to return the investment in three years." This claim was originally made in 1946 as an estimate. If the then existing total investment in steam motive power of $1.8 billion were to be replaced with diesels, the savings were estimated to be $55 million. The claim has been repeated each year since. In 1957, with but 69 per cent of the 1946 traffic, with its required diesel motive power, which had become an investment of $3.9 billion, it would have indicated a saving of $1 billion. Mr. Brown, in his paper, estimated diesel operation, (including an estimated 6.6 per cent savings with yard

diesel motive power) cost the railroads over $28 million more than equivalent modern steam power might have cost in 1957.

7. "They had saved the U.S. railways from bankruptcy, and had enabled the railways to increase their dividend payments since 1935." Did diesels save the New Haven Railroad from bankruptcy in 1961? U.S. railroads in general are now worse off financially than at anytime except during the Great Depression, because of lack of traffic which has nothing to do with motive power.

The claim that diesels attracted more shippers and passengers is ludicrous. Who cares whether his goods are hauled by one 2-10-4 or four GP-9's? Passenger and freight traffic is still declining. The 80,000,000 tons of coal which steam locomotives once consumed annually, accounted for quite a few jobs in West Virginia and Kentucky; but these facts were ignored in diesel advertising.

Track damage was an important claim for dieselization. To quote E. L. Pardee, president of the National Railway Historical Society in a speech referring to steam power which he delivered in Baltimore in November 1960: ". . . they had to straighten 22,000 rails, (in one year on one railroad) nearly all of which were engine bent, . . . one engine, on one trip of 55 miles, damaged three track miles of 90-pound rail, three miles of 110-pound rail, and four miles of 130-pound rail." (Such track damage was the result of dynamic augment — the vertical pounding of a locomotive created by the action of the pistons and rods, which can be balanced only for one speed.) Mr. Pardee, in reference to an Atlantic Coast Line 4-8-4, continued: "motion pictures . . . disclosed that the engine wheels were actually bouncing on the rails." However, the I.C.C. study (pages 119-120; and in Appendix I, page 240), stated that the small diameter driving wheels of diesels also cause track damage. Increased slippage of diesel wheels creates more "burns," weakening rails. Mr. Brown, in his paper reports no change in the relative costs of maintenance-of-way and structures between the years 1940 and 1959.

While the diesel proponents were claiming their product hauled 10,000 to 15,000 ton trains (few trains are over 5,000 tons), Missabe's big Yellowstones, (page 38) in their last show of might in the late 1950's, singlehandedly rolled ore trains nearly 20,000 gross tons in weight!

194

Dieselmen frequently point to Norfolk & Western as their supreme accomplishment. N&W had built one of the finest fleets of modern steam locomotives in the world. There were 143 articulateds of the 2-8-8-2 and 2-6-6-4 types. Their 4-8-4's held down some of the finest on-time passenger train performances in the country, while perhaps the best steam switch engines ever built did the yard chores. (The last of their S-1 0-8-0's, No. 244, rolled out of Roanoke in 1953 as the last steam locomotive built for a common-carrier in the United States.) Six years later, N&W was totally diesel-powered and the last S-1 was awaiting the torch! Although their Roanoke shops built the N&W engines, they depended on suppliers for a myriad of vital parts: pumps, feedwater heaters, stokers, injectors, boiler staybolts, to name a few. All of these suppliers had discontinued their steam locomotive business several years before, leaving N&W no choice; when they needed more power to handle increased traffic, diesels had to be ordered. The combination of depleting reserves of spare parts and a new management cut short the lives of Norfolk & Western's modern steam locomotives when, in 1957, the decision to dieselize was made. The improvements in the already-phenomenal operating ratio of the N&W are probably more attributable to the business genius of the railroad's president, Stuart Saunders, than to the diesel roster, the purchase of which got the company into debt for the first time in its history.

The totally opposing view of dieselization in the U.S., which is held by railroad management, also refers to reliable statistics, and the ideas of Mr. John W. Barriger, president of the Pittsburgh & Lake Erie (NYC), who is respected as one of the nation's foremost authorities on railway economics, are worth pondering. When asked by the author if diesel locomotives have saved the railroads money, Mr. Barriger replied: "Any rail profits realized since World War II are the result of diesel power." He also contends that diesel operations have saved the carriers one billion dollars.

Freeman Hubbard, editor of *Railroad Magazine,* wrote a provocative editorial in the August, 1961 issue entitled "Why do the Railroads buy Diesel Locomotives?" After mentioning the criminal indictment filed against General Motors Corporation for "monopolizing the production and sale of diesel locomotives," he delved behind the immediate charges leveled by Attorney General Robert F. Kennedy, and provided some thoughts as to why the railroads dieselized in the first place, scrapping thousands of modern steam engines in their prime of life. Mr. Hubbard quoted the indictment in reference to the vast amount of freight (12 million tons, January to September, 1960) shipped by GM; "because of this huge volume, the Corporation was able virtually to *order* railroads to buy its locomotives." By 1960 Electro-Motive Division of General Motors had turned out 84.1 per cent of all diesel locomotives manufactured in the United States. EMD contends that since they have sold the greater number of diesels, their product is superior to other diesels.

On the Electro-Motive indictment, John W. Barriger also offered some knowledgeable insight. He maintains that GM diesels are so superior to other diesels that they naturally dominate the market. As to the charges in the indictment, Mr. Barriger, who once sold diesels for a competitor of GM, calls them "pure bunk," and says that GM's "hands are perfectly clean." He has volunteered his presence as a witness for the defense in the trial.

These sharply conflicting points of view from reliable sources in railway economics and motive power, leave the situation so confused that an objective observer can arrive at no definite conclusions — even if the government were to win its case against General Motors. All arguments, accusations and claims fade in light of the great fact of railroading now and in the future; the steam locomotive is gone beyond the limits of all recall, and since the carriers have spent billions of dollars on the changeover of their motive power and servicing facilities, there is little prospect of a reciprocating steam locomotive ever being constructed for service on a Class One railroad.

Regardless of future indictments, types of motive power, engineering papers, politics and accusations, the issue will probably never be resolved to the satisfaction of all parties in this great railroad debate. However, H. F. Brown's reply to his critics must, of necessity, cast doubt upon any ultimate conclusions; "the comparative analysis made in the paper showed [the diesel's] economic performance to be about on a par with that of steam on its overall application to the United States Railways — no better, no worse."

STEAM LOCOMOTIVE TECHNOLOGY

During the century and a quarter in which the steam engine gloried in her dominance of the high iron, over 200,000 locomotives saw service on United States railroads. While the exact number is unknown, it is significant to note that approximately 25,000 steam engines puffed onto the Pennsylvania's roster during this period, and the Baldwin Locomotive Works constructed its 60,000th steam engine before the Great Depression.

In addition to the most common type of single-expansion rod-driven locomotive, described in detail on the following pages, the flexibility of compressed steam as a source of power allowed for many successful variations on its use. One of the most common departures from the "orthodox" locomotive was the double-expansion type, known as the "Mallet." The Mallet concept, named for its inventor, a French engineer, found its greatest acceptance on huge articulated freight locomotives in the United States during the first three decades of the 20th century. The principle involved here was as follows: rather than use steam once and exhaust it into the atmosphere while it still retained much of its force, it was exhausted instead, into a pair of low pressure cylinders which operated another set of driving wheels. This system sometimes proved inadequate and the low pressure cylinders were often so large (up to a 48-inch bore) that they created mechanical problems. Many Mallets had by-pass valves which enabled the engineer to operate the whole locomotive "simple," i.e., at high pressure, when necessary. Invariably, the front engine of a compound articulated contained the low pressure cylinders. By the mid-1930's the simple articulated became the vogue and virtually all of the modern articulateds operated on four high pressure cylinders of equal stroke and diameter. One of the marvelously efficient exceptions to this trend was Norfolk & Western's Y-6 series of compound 2-8-8-2's which were built right up until 1952, three years after any other railroad bought its last articulated. With few exceptions beside N&W, however, U. S. railroads went simple on their heavy power after 1930. (Turn to page 58 for a picture of N&W's Y-6, showing the 39-inch-diameter low-pressure cylinders).

Samuel Vauclain, the great designer of the Baldwin Locomotive Works originated the "Vauclain Compound," which was first applied to locomotives having one set of driving wheels before 1900. One of the most sophisticated designs utilizing the compound principle was a weird 4-8-0 built by American Locomotive Co. for the Delaware & Hudson. This was a triple-expansion engine which first worked steam in a high-pressure cylinder on the right rear, then sent it to an intermediate cylinder on the left rear. From there the steam was exhausted into

STEAM LOCOMOTIVE BUILDERS

There were many manufacturers during the 124 years in which steam locomotives were built for U. S. railroads. The earliest engines came from England, but it wasn't long before yankee ingenuity got into the act and by the mid-1850's, five companies were turning out 150 locomotives annually in Paterson, New Jersey, which had become the locomotive center of the U. S. After the Civil War, Philadelphia became the hub of activity of steam manufacture, and remained so until the last days. The largest commercial builders were Baldwin, American and Lima (which first entered the business by manufacturing Shays), as well as Porter, who was best known for small switch engines. Many famous 19th Century builders including Rogers, Cooke, Norris and others were absorbed by the larger firms or went out of business. A number of railroads, notably Pennsylvania and Norfolk & Western, built their own locomotives. Below are the builders' plates of (*left to right*) American, Baldwin and Pennsylvania Railroad.

a pair of low-pressure cylinders located in the usual place — under the smokebox.

Another unusual type of engine was the "fireless cooker" or "thermos bottle." Instead of boilers, locomotives of this type had heavily insulated steam storage tanks above their drivers. Steam was piped into the engine from a fixed boiler, usually at an industrial plant, and used when needed. Sometimes these smokeless engines could run ten hours without a "refill" of steam.

The ungraded roadbeds, poor quality track, sharp curves and inferior engineering often associated with logging and mining railroads bred an entire stable of geared iron horses. The first, most common, and most successful, was the Shay geared engine or "sidewinder." Named for its inventor, Ephraim Shay, this amazingly rugged and adaptable engine has become the most numerous of surviving steam engines in active service. The Shay's three cylinders were all mounted vertically on the right side. They drove a horizontal shaft which was geared to the wheels. All wheels are drive wheels under a Shay, thus they are identified by the number of trucks under the engine. Small Shays are usually two-truck engines, while the larger ones normally have a separate water tank, which is mounted on a powered third truck. Shays are very slow, with a top speed seldom exceeding 15 mph, and very powerful. The chief disadvantage of the Shay is its tendency to pound the rail under the right side, while passing comparatively lightly over the left rail.

The Climax, whose cylinders activated its wheels through the agency of a crankshaft mounted crosswise beneath the boiler, which

---

GEARED DRIVING MECHANISMS

At *right,* from top down, are shown in detail the driving mechanisms of the Shay, Heisler and Climax. Note that each photo is taken from approximately the same angle and that each shows the cylinders, shaft, and front truck. A similar shaft runs to the rear trucks. At the *lower right,* a Porter fireless 0-6-0 near the North American Rayon Corp. plant in Elizabethton, Tennessee. In the background, ET&WNC 2-8-0 No. 207. This is probably the last place in the United States where steam locomotives under separate ownership still work together in revenue service. Another Porter fireless — an 0-4-0 built in 1947 — still operates around the Connecticut Coke Co. in New Haven.

was geared to a center shaft leading to the trucks, was easier on track, but the least popular of the "big three" geared engines.

The Heisler, second in popularity only to the Shay, had two cylinders which were mounted vertically on either side of the boiler and canted inward, resulting in a "V" drive similar to an internal combustion engine. This arrangement turned a center shaft which was geared to one axle on each truck. A connecting rod from the primary wheels turned the secondary wheels. This resulted in less gearing, which the Heisler Company contended meant less maintenance, since the gearing was the most vulnerable mechanism in all three types. There are still a few Heislers in service, and at least two Climaxes.

The modern steam engine was an aggregation of complex mechanisms, whose operation is illustrated below. The drawing is of a hypothetical locomotive, but typical of steam power constructed in the 1920's and '30's.

The operation is as follows: The fuel (in this case, coal) enters the firebox through an automatic stoker, or by hand, through the fire doors (1). Water is fed into the boiler by means of an injector (2). After being burned in the firebox (3), the hot gases travel at tremendous speed through the boiler tubing (4), heating the water en route to the smokebox

(5). The heavy arrows indicate the direction the water takes as it flows around the tubes and over the firebox. The light arrows indicate the route of the gases from combustion to the stack (6). Arrow (7) indicates the live steam inlet to the valve chest and (8) the exhaust steam outlet. The valve (9) regulates the flow of steam to the cylinder. Steam exerting pressure moves the piston (10) and piston rod (11) which is attached to the crosshead (12). This mass of steel is held in place by the crosshead guides (13). The locomotive is reversed by admitting steam to the opposite side of the piston through the manipulation of the power reverse mechanism and the valve gear (in this case Walschaerts). The parts of the valve gear are as follows: valve stem (14), combination lever (15), radius bar (16), link (17), reverse gear (18), and the reverse lever (19) in the cab. The main rod (20) is the connection between the crosshead and the driving wheels. Connecting rods (21) extend from the main driver (22) to the other drivers. The eccentric crank and eccentric rod (23) also join the main driver and are attached to the main pin along with the connecting rod and main rod. Large counterbalancing weights (24) serve to neutralize the unequal weight of the rods which are attached to the wheels by means of connecting

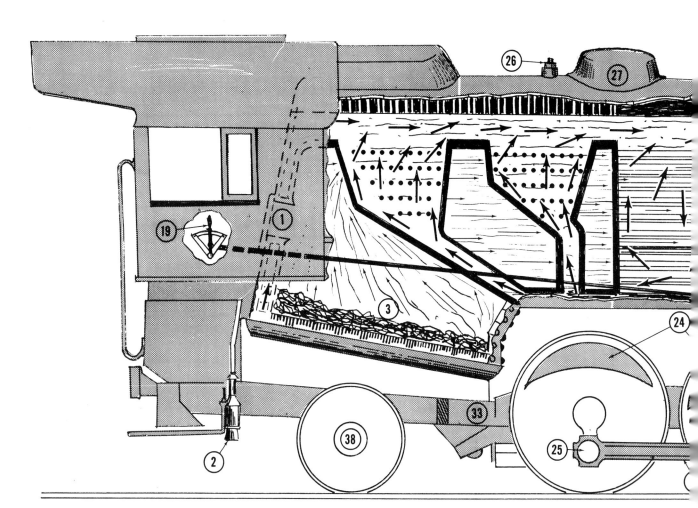

pins (25). The safety valves (26), steam dome (27), sand box (28) and bell (29) are located on top of the boiler. The generator (30) is steam operated and supplies electricity to the headlight (31), marker lights (32) and cab and tender lights. The frame (33) is a major sub-assembly which runs the entire length of the engine. The smokebox door (34) provides ready access into the front end for maintenance purposes. The pilot coupler (35) is mounted above the pilot, or cowcatcher (36). The pilot wheel assembly (37) is also called the pony truck or engine truck. The trailing truck (38) is sometimes referred to as the firebox truck.

LOCOMOTIVE INJECTOR

In addition to the running gear, there were other complex mechanisms inherent in the modern steam locomotive, such as airpumps, automatic stokers, feedwater heaters and various exhaust systems. At *right* is a diagram of the relatively small (No. (2) *below*) but vital injector; the mechanism by which cold water from the tender is admitted to the boiler which contains steam which may be as hot as 700 degrees Fahrenheit. If the water were sent into the locomotive cold, it could cause a geyser-like eruption back in the tender from the pressure. This particular injector is a Sellers Type S, and through the valves illustrated, mixed live steam with the incoming water, propelling both into the boiler.

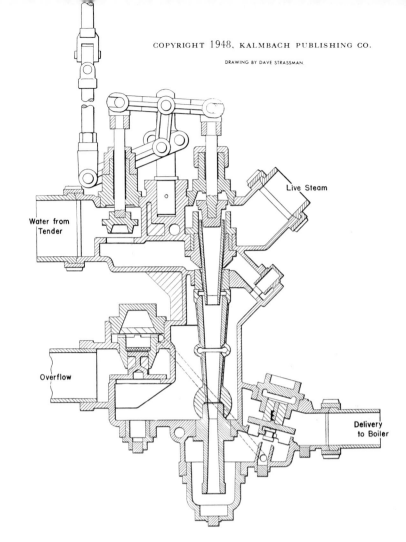

Live Steam

Water from Tender

Overflow

Delivery to Boiler

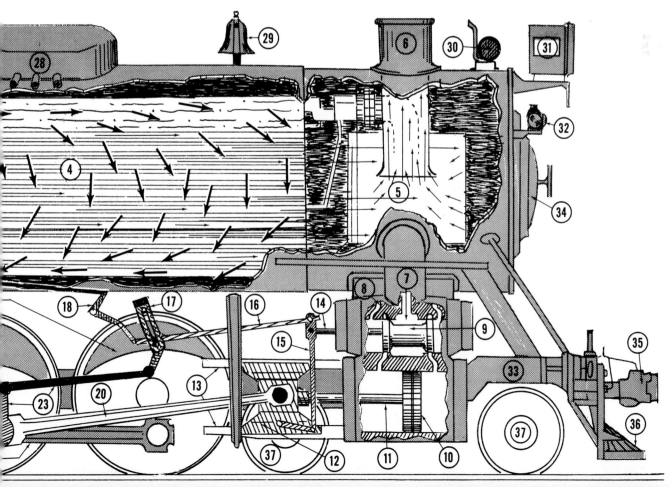

There were many different wheel arrangements applied to steam locomotives in the U. S., ranging from narrow gauge 0-4-0 tank engines weighing about nine tons, up to 650-ton articulateds which may have spread their weight over as many as 15 axles. Basically, freight engines had smaller driving wheels than passenger, and passenger engines were usually lighter and had a four-wheel pilot truck. Switch engines were characterized by a lack of pilot wheels and usually, no trailing axle. A (T) after a designation indicates that tank engines were common in this wheel arrangement.

4-4-0 American. Most popular dual service type of 19th century.

4-6-0 Ten-wheeler. Originally freight, later dual service.

4-8-0 Twelve-wheeler. Some modern 4-8-0's still active in Mexico.

4-10-0 Mastodon. Few built for U. S. railroads.

4-4-2 Atlantic. First built 1895 for ACL. Popular passenger engine until 1920's

4-6-2 Pacific. First U. S. road to use it was M. P. in 1903.

4-8-2 Mountain (N. Y. C. Mohawk). C&O first used it in 1911, dual service.

4-10-2 Southern Pacific. Named for the road which originated it.

4-12-2 Union Pacific. Largest non-articulated prior to W. W. II.

4-4-4 Reading (CPR Jubilee). Reading engines had first four wheel trailing truck

4-6-4 Hudson. Built for N. Y. C. in 1927. N. Y. C. had 275 built by 1937.

4-8-4 Northern. Dual service. First built in 1927. Had at least seven names.

2-6-0 Mogul. First built 1863. Most popular freight engine of 19th century.

2-8-0 Consolidation. Built for L.V.R.R., 1866. Most common locomotive.

2-10-0 Decapod. Built for L.V.R.R., 1868.

2-4-2 Columbia. A rare type in the United States.

2-6-2 Prairie. Popular passenger engine around 1900.

2-8-2 Mikado. 1893. First to lift firebox above drivers.

2-10-2 Santa Fe (I.C. Central). First built in 1903 for AT&SF.

2-6-4 Adriatic. Little use in U. S. Quite popular in Europe.

2-8-4 Berkshire (C&O Kanawha, I. C. Lima) First built for Boston & Albany.

2-10-4 Texas (CB&Q Colorado, CNR Selkirk). Built for T&P in 1925.

2-6-6-0 Built for Virginian. World's largest before 1903.

2-8-8-0 Quite popular as a helper or slow freight engine.

2-6-6-2 Built in 1903 for B&O. Still active in Mexico.

2-8-8-2 Last Mallets built in U. S. (N&W Y-6b, 1952).

2-10-10-2 Used by Virginian to haul 17,000 ton trains.

2-6-6-4 First built in 1935 for P.&W.Va.

2-8-8-4 Yellowstone. Built 1925 for N. P.

2-6-6-6 Allegheny. Built 1941 for C&O.

4-8-8-2 Articulated-Consolidation. S. P. had 195 of these cab-forwards.

4-6-6-4 Challenger. Developed by U. P. in 1936.

4-8-8-4 Big Boy. Developed by U. P. in 1941. World's largest.

0-4-0(T) Switch engine.

0-6-0(T) Switch engine.

0-8-0 Switch engine.

0-10-0 Used in early 1900's. Few built after 1920.

0-6-2(T) Rare switch engine type.

0-10-2 Union. Built 1936 for Union R.R. Heaviest switchers.

0-4-2(T) Popular narrow gauge type.

0-4-4(T) Popular narrow gauge type.

Some of the earliest locomotives had wheel arrangements such as: 4-2-4, 6-2-0, 2-2-0, 4-2-0, 2-4-0. Major railroads built many modern experimentals, including 4-4-4-4, 4-4-6-4, 4-6-4-4, 6-4-4-6, 6-8-6 in late 1930's and '40's. (The T-1 4-4-4-4 and Q-1 4-4-6-4 of the Pennsylvania actually were produced in impressive numbers until the late '40's).

A CENTURY OF PROGRESS

The cab of the steam locomotive underwent as great a change as did the exterior appearance since the Civil War era. The backheads of the Baltimore & Ohio's *William Mason* (*left*) and a modern articulated (*below*) dramatically illustrate the vast complexities wrought by increased size, modernization and automation of many of the functions of steam crewmen. The engineer of 1860 had only to cope with a throttle, a Johnson bar (reverse lever), an injector valve, a steam pressure gauge and a water level gauge, plus, of course, the bell and whistle cords. The fireman had to cope with a shovel (or cord wood). Things were different eighty years later. Both photos are approximately the same scale.

Courtesy Railroad Magazine

"IN THE SUMMER THE ENGINEER ROASTED; IN THE WINTER THE FIREMAN FROZE."

The Camelback, or Mother Hubbard, was once a common type of locomotive on such roads as the Jersey Central, the Reading, the Lackawanna, and the New York, Ontario & Western, as well as others. There are only three of these center-cab engines preserved — a Lackawanna 4-4-0 at the Museum of Transport, CNJ's refurbished 4-4-2, No. 592, at the B&O Museum, and a famous little 0-4-0 switcher, which as late as 1962, would putter down to the Reading right-of-way at Birdsboro, Pennsylvania, to exchange whistle salutes with that road's T-1 4-8-4's. The wide Wootten fireboxes on these locomotives limited

visibility to such a degree that the cab was built astride the boiler, leaving the engineer in a cramped, filthy and hot location (*above left*) and the fireman on an exposed, lonely and dangerous deck (*above right*). Several thousand of these engines were built in virtually every common wheel arrangement between the 1870's and 1918. The 0-4-0 shown here is the last active Camelback. She was built by Baldwin for the Reading in 1903, and until recently, worked for the Colorado Fuel & Iron Company. Her continued operation is assured by her new owner, the Strasburg Rail Road, which uses her to switch around the Strasburg yard.

THE LAST FIRES ARE DROPPED

Above, left, Kentucky & Tennessee 2-8-2 No. 11 spends a dreary day in the snug comfort of the engine house in Stearns, Ky. *Below,* on a late summer afternoon in Dundon, West Virginia, Consolidation No. 14 of the Buffalo Creek and Gauley

moves out of the yard while the road's two other 2-8-0's await future assignments. *Above,* now in storage to back-up Bevier & Southern's new diesel, Burlington 2-8-2 No. 4963 may eventually join her celebrated sister, No. 4960, in fantrip service.

The last days of mainline steam were charged with alternate moods of expectation and despair for the embattled fans who had come to love the big locomotives. As the final cataclysm of the late '50's crashed down upon the cult of steam, the fans, armed with film and recording tape, were everywhere to preserve the lingering downfall.

The seekers of steam were amazed by the squalid disrepair into which the last locomotives had fallen; for motive-power superintendents were not disposed to spend money on engines which would not survive the next diesel delivery. So it was in 1956, when a decrepit Pennsy M-1, her keystone plate already gone, was among a number of engines withdrawn from scrap-lines to aid in a traffic upsurge. The P.R.R. had phased out steam so fast that it had to rent 10 Reading 4-8-4's during this crisis!

Out west, the beautiful GS-series locomotives which the Espee so proudly ran at the head-end of its *Daylights* wound up their service on commuter runs. During their final months, Union Pacific's 800's were allowed to acquire a covering of dirt and grime which would have shocked officials several years earlier. During this time it was speculated that when Big Boy no longer did battle with the grade at Sherman, the end of steam would indeed have come. This prophecy was terribly correct, for within a few months after the last 4000 dropped its fires at Green River, Class One steam had disappeared entirely from the rails — to be recalled only for fan trips.

In the early '60's a record such as this could still be compiled, but even as these survivors were being sought out, the carnage persisted. By 1963 only a fraction of the active engines pictured here remained on the rails. This book was prepared at the last hour. Any future comprehensive pictorial record of the workaday steam locomotive in North America will have to treat it as academic history.

Most railroads dispatched their retired engines to the torch in the manner of the Southern: "quietly, quickly and mercilessly," as reported in *The Georgian Locomotive*. The future appeared even bleaker for the approximately 100 revenue steam engines to survive to the mid-1960's. Bevier & Southern had just dieselized; Brooklyn Eastern District Terminal steam was doomed; rumors of the Kentucky & Tennessee and the Brimstone contemplating dieselization were confirmed. The final siege had begun when, in late 1962, N de M sent the first of its 4-8-4's to the torch. The rest would follow quickly.

The only consolations were that the Rio Grande had at last given up attempts to abandon the Silverton Branch, that a number of tourist lines were flourishing, and that a few of the short lines had stockpiled enough spare parts to keep operating a few more years. Overseas the picture was somewhat brighter. In many countries, existing steam locomotives would probably remain in service for many years, and the railways of India placed orders for 126 brand-new steam locomotives.

So it was, that the great means to empire saddened many by her silent passing. As she slowly backed off the mainline of history and disappeared through the weed-grown meadows of the branch-line to oblivion, the steam locomotive took more than the fond memories of millions to her valhalla. An era of Americana, and the excitement and great accomplishments associated with that glory time rode with her. It may truly be said that the long night of the railroad industry was indeed symbolized by the twilight of the steam locomotive.

Opposite, Mobile & Gulf Mogul No. 97, a beautiful Baldwin of classical proportions, rests from her labors in the Autumn of 1962 in Alabama. *Right,* the 'Possum Trot Line's thrice-weekly mixed hightails back toward Reader, Arkansas, after sunset with tank cars of asphalt for the Missouri Pacific.

The photography work for *The Twilight of Steam Locomotives* was happily uncomplex. Filters and fancy lenses were completely alien to this venture. Two twin-lens 2¼" reflexes, a Yashica-Mat and a Minolta Autocord, a light meter by day and a tripod by night, were the only equipment used. Kodak's Plus-X, Panatomic-X, and Tri-X films were equal to the black and white chores, as were Adox, Varipan and a few rolls of Perutz film. Ektachrome Professional film supplied slides of good quality for the color reproductions.

Recommended Reading, Recordings

In recent years, there has been an abundance of publications dealing with the steam locomotive and its role in American railroading. The most celebrated of these are a series of books by Lucius Beebe, the one rail historian who has gained a national reputation as such. The following is a listing of those books which, in the author's opinion best convey the age of steam. They include technical and historical works, folklore, and — in the case of *The Georgian Locomotive,* an abstract departure into the previously unwritten subject of the influences of architectural and artistic concepts in steam engine design. Some of the best LP recordings are also listed.

BOOKS

Mixed Train Daily, Lucius Beebe, E. P. Dutton & Co., Inc., 1947. *Steam's Finest Hour,* David P. Morgan, Kalmbach Publishing Co., 1959. A *Treasury of Railroad Folklore,* B. A. Botkin and Alvin F. Harlow, Crown Publishers, 1953. *Railroad Avenue,* Freeman Hubbard, McGraw-Hill, 1945. *Trains,* Robert Selph Henry, Bobbs-Merrill Co., 1934. *Canadian Steam!,* David P. Morgan, Kalmbach Publishing Co., 1961. *The Age of Steam,* Lucius Beebe, Rinehart & Co., 1957. *The Georgian Locomotive,* H. Stafford Bryant, Jr., Barre Gazette, 1962. *Slow Train to Yesterday,* Archie Robertson, Houghton-Mifflin, 1945. *The Last of Steam,* Joe G. Collins, Howell-North Books, 1960.

RECORDS

These records are listed according to producers. Most of them, notably Mobile Fidelity, North Jersey, and O. Winston Link (the photographer who acquired national acclaim for his night work on the Norfolk & Western) have other albums of superior quality on the market. North Jersey: *Reading 2124* (volume I & II), *Rio Grande to Silverton.* O. Winston Link; *The Fading Giant* (Sounds of Steam Railroading, vol. II), *Thunder on Blue Ridge* (Sounds of Steam Railroading, vol. III). Mobile Fidelity: *Remember When?, Whistling thru Dixie, Steam Railroading Under Thundering Skies* (the last is of exceptional interest). RLP Company: *Steam Along the Chicago & Northwestern.* Stan Kistler: *Whistles in the Woods.*

MAGAZINES

There are two circulating fan magazines of varied content and interest. *Railroad Magazine* is published bi-monthly by Popular Publications, Inc., New York, and is a good source of motive power rosters, railroad lore and stories in addition to good articles on the rail industry in general and steam in particular. *Trains,* published by Kalmbach of Milwaukee, is a slick-paper publication which deals more with the business end of railroading, from the railfan angle. There has been an excellent series of illustrated articles on the greatest U. S. steam engines and the annual "all-steam" issue is very informative. It is published monthly. The great variety in content, editorial policy and format make both magazines worthwhile reading, and most fans who read one also read the other.

End Sheet: The Summit at Cumbres Pass

*"For one Moment in Eternity...
a Machine at once useful and beautiful."*
—Lucius Beebe